Pixar with Lacan

Pixar with Lacan

The Hysteric's Guide to Animation

Lilian Munk Rösing

Bloomsbury Academic
An imprint of Bloomsbury Publishing Inc

B L O O M S B U R Y
NEW YORK • LONDON • OXFORD • NEW DELHI • SYDNEY

Bloomsbury Academic
An imprint of Bloomsbury Publishing Inc

1385 Broadway
New York
NY 10018
USA

50 Bedford Square
London
WC1B 3DP
UK

www.bloomsbury.com

BLOOMSBURY and the Diana logo are trademarks of Bloomsbury Publishing Plc

First published 2016
Paperback edition first published 2017

Library of Congress Cataloging-in-Publication Data

Rösing, Lilian Munk, 1967- author.
Pixar with Lacan : the hysteric's guide to animation / Lilian Munk Rösing.
pages cm
Summary: "Presents Lacanian interpretations of the animations films from Pixar Studio with the double aim of analysing an influential filmic oeuvre of contemporary popular culture and giving an introduction to Lacanian cultural analysis"—Provided by publisher.
Includes bibliographical references and index.
ISBN 978-1-62892-059-8 (hardback)
1. Animated films—United States—History and criticism. 2. Pixar (Firm)
3. Lacan, Jacques, 1901-1981. I. Title.
NC1766.U52P5838 2015
791.43′340973—dc23
2015022830

ISBN: HB: 978-1-6289-2059-8
PB: 978-1-5013-2017-0
ePub: 978-1-6289-2062-8
ePDF: 978-1-6289-2061-1

Typeset by RefineCatch Limited, Bungay, Suffolk, UK

For Aron and Josef

Contents

Introduction

The technique of animated films seems to carry within it, as a kind of meta-reflection, the very philosophical problem of 'animation'. What does it take to 'animate' a thing or an animal? That is, what is 'a soul' (Latin: 'animus')? How is something 'humanized'? Psychoanalytically speaking, how is the subject constituted? What makes the subject tick, what animates the human subject (as different from the thing or the animal)? Pixar's animated universe seems to me not only to present its creators with this problem, but also to have it as a recurring theme. Or, put another way: the problem of 'animation' seems to expand from being a problem of production to defining to a large degree the themes and stories of the films. In the terms of animation theorist Alan Cholodenko, animation is here both 'trope' and 'device' (Cholodenko 2007: 60).

The rat in *Ratatouille* is perhaps the clearest image of this. The film is about a rat who installs himself in the toque of a kitchen boy, pulling his hair like the puppeteer pulls the strings of his puppet, directing him to cook delicious dishes gaining him the reputation of a master chef. The central image of the whole story is thus a kind of imaginative answer to the question: What animates the human being, what is his soul? The answer is – a rat!

Pixar's very first feature film, *Toy Story*, is not just about living toys, but about toys becoming alive. That is, again, the characters are not just animated toys, the process of animating them becomes a part of the story, the question of what animates them becomes an important theme. At first animated by the child's play, which thus becomes a kind of allegory of the animators' work, they soon show themselves to be animated by gaze and voice. The fantasy of toys becoming alive is not only what created the film, but also, in *Toy Story*, a decisive part of the plot, used to conquer the villain.

This self-reflexivity of animation was one of Sergei Eisenstein's important points in his enthusiastic notes on Disney from the 1940s. Eisenstein saw how Disney's cartoons were 'animated twice': both in the sense of making drawings come alive, and in the sense of animating, that is humanizing, the animals that were the characters (Eisenstein 2011: 43).

This duplicity of animation – technique and theme, device and trope – may explain why animation's characters are prototypically animals and things being 'animated' into humans. As the animation historian Donald Crafton observes about 'the normally inanimate objects of everyday life – furniture, tools, toys' that were the subjects of animation from its early days: 'These subjects, then, however "haunted", were also representations of animators' enduring concern with autokinesis, movement in itself, the stuff of animation.' Crafton's point is that the animated thing from one (animist) point of view is 'haunted', but from another (mechanist) view rather reflects the technical inventions of the turn-of-the-century, the automobile and the aeroplane: 'objects moving with what seemed their own internal life.' (Crafton 1982: 32). The zone where soul and mechanics meet, comically or uncannily, will in this book be a meeting place for animation and psychoanalysis.

The most difficult figure to construct in computer animation is apparently the human figure. In the beginning of Pixar's story of developing the technique of computer animation, the flexibility, skin and face of the human body presented the animators with great difficulties. 'Human characters are difficult to present in our medium', as director Jan Pinkava puts it on the commentary track to the early Pixar short film *Geri's Game*. This technical difficulty in constructing a human being highlights the question of what a human being is.

Pixar has been leading in developing the technique of computer animation. They have had enormous success in animating the inanimate, constructing the human. Their films will be the object of analysis in this book, taking its point of departure from the interest that Pixar shares with psychoanalysis: What distinguishes the human subject from animals and things?

What animates the subject, according to Pixar? What animates the subject, according to psychoanalysis? These two questions will be examined in parallel in the following analyses of Pixar's films. It will be shown how the human subject is animated by desire, language, gaze and voice, but also how these distinctive human features paradoxically even function as some kind of alien mechanism in the subject.

The alien in control

One of the first Pixar shorts, *Red's Dream* (John Lasseter, 1987), a remarkable mixture of slapstick and film noir, is about the unicycle Red standing in the corner in a bike shop, on sale. The unicycle is provided with a mind as the camera dives into its saddle and shows us the dream going on there. He dreams that he is in the circus underneath a juggling clown in front of an audience, and that he detaches himself from the clown and starts juggling himself. Again, Pixar not only gives us an animated unicycle, but the very process or scene of its being gradually animated, culminating in the prop taking over the agency of the human performer.

In *Red's Dream* the unicycle is animated by three things: dreaming, juggling and having an audience. These seem to correspond to some of the important principles that psychoanalysis presumes to animate the human subject. As Sigmund Freud argued in his *Traumdeutung*, dreams are the 'royal road' to the unconscious, which is finally what animates the human subject. The repetitive, mechanical activity of juggling has the dynamics of that compulsion to repeat what Freud named 'the death drive'. And finally, the audience is what Jacques Lacan would call 'the big Other', the gaze before which we perform our lives, also when we are completely solitary. The feeling of being watched, of being the object of some kind of perception that knows what we want and how we ought to be and behave, is what Lacan calls by the name of 'the big Other'.

The clown in *Red's Dream* was, according to the commentary track, one of the first organic forms made by Pixar. Finally, one might wonder whether the clown does not seem somehow more mechanical, more thing-like than the unicycle. As a collision between the mechanical and the living he has something of the Bergsonian comic about him. To Bergson the application of something mechanical to the supple and living has a comic effect (Bergson 1999: 39). But then again, the mechanical dimension expressed in the monotonous juggling may very much be the very drive that animates the human being, the compulsion to repeat.

On the commentary track to *Red's Dream* we hear from director John Lasseter that he is proud of the end, because it has the 'pathos' that according to his mentors at Disney should be put into animation. Finally, being animated also means being moved, as Sianne Ngai points out when defining 'animatedness' (or 'innervation, agitation') as 'one of the most basic ways in which affect becomes socially recognizable in the age of mechanical reproducibility', implying 'the most basic or minimal of all affective conditions: that of being moved' (Ngai 2005: 91).

In a later short film, *Lifted* (Gary Rydstrom, 2006), the theme of animation is obvious; the film is about a sleeping man being animated by green aliens from a UFO, and from the commentary track it is clear that this theme also has the meta-level of referring to the work that goes into the making of animated films.

The film is instructed by Gary Rydstrom, a famous sound-guy at Pixar, and on the commentary track he explains how he sees it as an allegory of his own career, identifying himself with the student alien Stu who is sweating at the mixing console, supervised by his instructor Mr B. In a highly comical plot Stu really has problems directing the beams that are to lift up the sleeping man into the UFO, and when he finally succeeds, he lets go of the button too early, sending the man back to earth again. The farmer animated by aliens seems a perfect illustration of Slavoj Žižek's dictum, pronounced in Sophie Fiennes' documentary *The Pervert's Guide to Cinema*: 'Humanity means the alien is controlling our animal body.' The soul is an alien.

From the example of those short films we can deduce the animating principle as suspended between what Lacan would call 'the big Other' and a kind of non-human mechanics that defines the human at its very core. Let us illuminate this by diving a little more into the idea of animation implied in psychoanalysis and more explicitly conceptualized in theorists inspired by psychoanalysis.

Animated by the Other

We are living in times when the dominance of natural science tends to wipe out the distinction between human and animal. Human beings are regarded as working machines that can be repaired by medicine and cognitive therapy if they do not function. Or they are seen as animals whose strivings, choices and acts can be understood from the principle of sustaining the existence of the individual as well as of the species.

To psychoanalysis, the distinction between human and animal remains crucial. What Freud discovered was exactly that the human is the being whose choices and acts often seem to run completely counter to self-sustainment. The human being is the survival of the misfit. To psychoanalysis, the human subject is primarily animated by desire. And desire is something different from (animal) need. The human is the being who will turn every need into a desire as soon as it is just minimally fulfilled. Hunger is for instance a need, while the want for well-cooked dishes and new exciting tastes is a desire. The rat protagonist in *Ratatouille* distinguishes himself from his fellow rats exactly by his passion for cooking.

To be a being of desire also means to be a being of language, a *parlêtre* as Jacques Lacan calls it ('parler' = speak, 'être' = being). The human child is inscribed into language and desire at the same moment, the moment that Freud calls 'the Oedipus complex', while Jacques Lacan calls it 'the symbolic castration'. This is the basic moment of separation from which desire and language are born: you neither desire, nor name an object until you are separated from it. The cardinal example would be the mother, both as a thing (that you can desire when separated from it) and as a word (by which you will not call her before separation).

With an important term from Jacques Lacan, to be a being of language and desire also means to be a being relating to the Other. One of Lacan's definitions of 'the Other' is 'the subject supposed to know'. That is, the person or instance that I imagine to know the truth about me (who I really am and what I really want), be it God, my shrink, my boyfriend, a political party, Jacques Lacan or a more diffuse set of norms and values. At its broadest 'the Other' means the whole symbolic order, the order of society and language, naming and identifying me.

My desire is defined through my relating to the Other. 'Man's desire is the desire of the Other', writes Lacan (1979: 235), meaning both that man desires the Other, and that his desire is somehow the Other's desire. Lacan goes on to say that 'the Other's question' is 'Che Vuoi?', Italian for: 'What do you want?' This, in Mozart's opera, is Don Giovanni's question to the paternal statue that comes to judge him, but in Lacan's use it is just as much the statue's, the Other's, question to Don Giovanni, the subject.

You may figure the Other in the image of the adult faces bending over the baby's cradle, raising in him the question 'What do they want?' meaning also 'What do they want me to want?' The fact that the subject desires what the Other wants him to desire becomes clear in the example of the child pleasing his parents by wanting what they want him to want ('Oh, you want to be a doctor, my son? I am pleased!'). Žižek's example is Anna Freud's dream of strawberries, recorded in Freud's *Interpretation of Dreams*. As a child Anna lies sleeping, recovering from a fever, and mumbles in her dream: 'Strawberries!' Žižek's point is that Anna hereby less expresses her desire for strawberries than fulfils her parents' desire for her to recover and desire strawberries; her desire is her parents' desire (Žižek 1997: 9).

The Other may be imagined as the gaze for which we perform our selves, our lives. The one I am posing for, even when all alone, is the imaginary camera. To psychoanalysis, the human being is thus also a creature of the gaze, and this is one reason why film may tell us something basic about *la condition humaine*. To Lacan, having a gaze actually does not mean to be in control of it, but rather to be exposed to the gaze of the big Other. My gaze is my response to the big Other, but what I am looking for is actually the big Other's gaze. I may feel recognized and desired by this gaze, having my image narcissistically affirmed. Or I may feel the paranoia of being watched, being surveyed. I may feel subject of my gaze, looking at pleasurable sights, for instance when going to the cinema. Or I may feel object of a vision, having my gaze exposed to something that I would rather not see, which is actually also a part of the cinematic experience, and has its primal image in the primal scene: the sight (or fantasy) of the parents having sex. The primal scene is also a figuration of the Other, of the 'Che Vuoi?' – What do you want (me to want)? – as it is an answer to the child's question: 'From which desire am I born?'

Lacanian film theory has lately undergone a change from focusing on the gaze as a form of control and imaginary identification to the gaze as something the subject is submitted to. In her famous and influential essay 'Visual Pleasure and Narrative Cinema' (1975) Laura Mulvey argues that the ideal spectator of the Hollywood film is male, controlling the objectified women on screen by his gaze. Todd McGowan, on the contrary, in *The Real Gaze* (2007) turns the focus from what he calls 'the imaginary look' (film as ideal images dictated by the dominating ideology, including ideal images of women dictated by patriarchy) to 'the real gaze' (cinema as the place where you can actually watch the fantasy of the Other staring back at you, which is always a very scary experience). We shall get back to this split of the gaze in the chapter on *Toy Story 2*.

In Pixar's films the Other animating the characters' desire is often a figure emanating from the screen. In *Ratatouille* it is the figure of the master chef Gusteau whom the rat Remy watches on the TV screen, thereby assuming his own desire to be a cook. In *Up* it is the figure of the adventurer Charles Muntz whom the protagonist Carl watches in the cinema as a small boy, thereby defining his own life's adventure. This reflects the fact of our culture that the film and TV industry functions as a big Other, as the one which tells us what to desire.

Pixar's *Up* stages the issue of the human/animal divide in the image of speaking dogs. The dogs' master has given them voices by providing them with electronic necklaces that somehow translate their thoughts into human speech. Thus, they are animated by their master's voice, and the film presents us with the question of whether their human language turns them into creatures of desire and their master into a figure of the big Other, or if they stay creatures of need, the master being the one who can fulfil their needs and condition their behaviour like some Pavlov. This will be discussed in detail in the chapter on *Up*, but I will premise the way that Renata Salecl distinguishes between dog and man exactly by invoking the big Other: 'In Pavlov's experiment the dog does not become troubled with the desire of the experimenter: Dogs do not question the desire of the Other. And this is what distinguishes them from human beings' (Salecl 2000: 113).

Animated by the surplus

To Eric Santner, inspired by psychoanalysis, human beings are animated by the 'surplus of life' that is created because they are 'beings of language, as animals compelled to live their lives in the field of the Other'. 'If beneath the skin there is more life than we have bargained for [like the wound in Kafka's Landartzt] this is because what we find there is not only tissue, blood, bones, nerves [. . .] but also the fleshy surplus we take on when we are taken in by the cultural, historical modes by which we are "naturalized"' (Santner 2011: 122).

At a certain moment, inspired by Georges Bataille, Eric Santner designates the 'surplus' animating man by the prefix 'super', man being thus a kind of 'superman'. I will get more into this in the chapter on Pixar's superhero film, *The Incredibles*, which is very much about the problem of dealing with your animating principle as some kind of troubling surplus.

Also to Santner it is important to distinguish human beings from animals. A fly may 'wriggle' in a way that makes it more humanoid than a thing. Thus Wittgenstein found it easier to ascribe feelings to a fly than to a stone. But Santner insists that the human 'twitching' or 'wriggling' is of another kind than that of the animal. And he honours Freud as the one who 'first grasped the *Urphänomen* of human wriggling in the uncanny body of his central European neurotics, a body whose flesh – and the biopolitical pressures it incarnated – he very much shared' (Santner 2011: 124). So to Santner the spasms in our human flesh are not caused by an animal principle, but by language and the Other, which animate us in a different way from animals.

The human 'flesh' is not the condition we share with the animal, but is created when we are inscribed in the symbolic order, when the subject (the sovereign) is *incarnated*. So human flesh is always an incarnation, always incarnating a position within the symbolic order. When the crown is squeezed on the king's head, or the hat on the pope's, his flesh is created (cf. Francis Bacon's famous *Study after Velazquez's Pope Innocent X* that illustrates Santner's point (Santner

2011: 139)). The human flesh is to Santner 'a spectral materiality [. . .] that forms at the impossible jointure of body and letter, soma and signifier, enjoyment and entitlement' (Santner 2011: 95).

Alan Cholodenko also links spectrality and animation. In his essay 'The Spectre in the Screen' (Cholodenko 2008) he refers this linking, which has in his earlier essays mainly been informed by Freud, Derrida and Baudrillard, to the rereading of Lacan by Slavoj Žižek, Joan Copjec and Todd McGowan, following the turn from the imaginary look to the real gaze. Cholodenko defines the 'animus' of animation rather as a spectre than a soul, proposing the Homeric term 'psuche' (the undead spectre) as an alternative to the Platonic 'psyche' (the immortal soul).

The materiality out of which human or humanoid bodies are made in computer animation may indeed be said to be 'a spectral materiality'. It will be this book's interest to examine how Pixar animates this spectral materiality in order to make it appear human.

Autonomy and automaton

Santner's concept of animation is a concept of undeadness. The repetition compulsion is animating our bodies, so that we confuse being alive with being undead, pulse with compulsion. The psychoanalytic cure is de-animation. 'The psychoanalytic cure (as well as ethical and political acts informed by Freud's discoveries) ought to be understood as a practice by means of which such nihilistic vitality would be deanimated' (Santner 2006: 81).

Finally, at its core, the desire that distinguishes the human subject is a purposeless compulsion to repeat. This is the truth about desire that Lacan takes from Freud's essay 'Beyond the Pleasure Principle'. Here Freud defines the death drive as the compulsion to repeat beyond any pleasure-seeking or self-preservation. To Lacan this drive beyond pleasure is actually at the core of desire, it is desire stripped of its symbolic and imaginary dressing, desire stripped of the words and images that make it pleasurable. Slavoj Žižek describes drive as 'a blind automatism of repetition beyond pleasure-seeking, self-preservation' and declares it to define 'la condition humaine as such' (Žižek 1989: 4–5). This takes us to the connection between animation and automaton. Being animated means both being lively and being mechanically controlled, as a puppet by a puppeteer. The animated figure is somewhere in between autonomy and automaton.

As Alan Cholodenko has shown, animation's sense of 'bringing to motion' relates the animated to the automatic. The automaton is that which is made to move by itself. Cholodenko relates the animation/automaton figure to the philosophical debate between animists and mechanists (Cholodenko 1991: 16). Looking at an animated thing, one could either stress the animistic feeling of thingness being endowed with human life, as does Sergei Eisenstein, or one could stress the mechanist side of something being technically brought to move by itself. 'Automaton', as defined by the dictionary, both means animated thing and a mechanized human being (cf. Cholodenko 2007: 502). Cholodenko's concept of 'the animatic' includes both the animation of the material and the mechanization of life, insisting on their interrelatedness, not only in the technique of animation, but also in the human being: 'Man is always already hybrid, "man-machine" – "animate inanimate"' (Cholodenko 2007: 494). I would like to expand this idea to include the Freudian death drive, understood as compulsion to repeat, as a mechanical and, so to speak, non-human drive at the core of humanity. Cholodenko does refer to the Freudian death drive, but in its meaning of 'the drive of animate beings to return to the inanimate state from which they came' (Cholodenko 2007: 504). Leaning on Lacan's and Žižek's interpretation of the death drive I rather regard it as a mechanism, a 'blind automatism' animating the subject. Though, if the death drive itself is both an animating principle and the drive towards de-animation, this actually supports Cholodenko's blurring of the dividing line between the mechanization of the animate and the animation of the inanimate. Thus death drive is similar to what Cholodenko terms 'lifedeath'.

The ambiguous zone of (mechanical) automatism and (human) autonomy is also a point in Rey Chow's essay 'Postmodern Automatons'. Here she points to the automatism *and* plasticity of animated characters as both a symptom of a capitalist working culture and a possible way of emancipation (Chow 1993). The automatism testifies to the working machine of Fordism (incarnated so brilliantly by Charlie Chaplin in *Modern Times*), but was also a device of the surrealist artists aimed at liberating the spontaneous surplus of the unconscious. The flexibility testifies to the adaptability demanded from the post-Fordist worker (supple subjection to power), but was also celebrated by Eisenstein, in his praise of Disney, as 'plasmaticness', the emancipatory potential to escape rigid forms (Ngai 2005: 100–1).

The double character of animation as automatic and autonomous motion is at stake in Pixar. When the lamb in the short film '*Boundin*' (Bud Luckey, 2003) is re-animated after his depression, he just 'bounds, bounds, bounds and rebounds', as the lyrics tell us, and the ever-bounding lamb becomes an image at once of some stupid automatism, and of freedom. The bounding at once seems toyish (resembling a toy animated by a spring) and human (the expression of joy). The animated things and animals are at once humanized non-humans and pointing to something non-human in human.

Perhaps animated things and animals can teach us about the specifically human not only as something that has to be added to non-human in order to humanize it, but also as something actually non-human, a certain induced mechanics or organ, at the core of human being. The dogs in *Up*, being animated by an electronic necklace that gives them a human voice, are an example: They show us the voice to be at once something specifically human and a kind of mechanics induced in the human being, as the dog's mechanical speech seems a reflection of the human boy protagonist's speech.

As an interaction between the lively and the mechanical, animation relates both to Henri Bergson's concept of the comical and Sigmund Freud's concept of the uncanny. The lamb's bounding, in between mechanical move and vital expression, the double exposure of a toy and a living creature, is comic. So is the mechanical talk of the dogs in *Up*. The comic effect of the characters in *Toy Story* may also relate not so much to the humanization of the toys as to their showing the toyish dimension of human beings, following Bergson's definition of the comical as the mechanization of the living. But the blending of the living and the mechanical is also an instance of Freud's definition of the uncanny. To Freud, it is uncanny when you find mechanics at the place where you expected to find a soul. This happens for instance in *Monsters, Inc.*, when the child asleep in his bed turns out to be a mechanical doll, constructed as a practising prop for the monster students who are taught how to scare children.

As Cholodenko points out, Freud links his concept of the 'uncanny' both to mechanizing the living and animating the dead (Cholodenko 2007: 503). Referring to the psychiatrist Ernst Jentsch, Freud lists 'constructed dolls and automata' as uncanny, followed by 'epileptic fits' and 'the impression of automatic, mechanical processes at work behind [. . .] mental activity' (Freud 1955c: 226). These are examples of the uncanny as finding mechanics where you expected to find life or soul. But Freud also relates the uncanny to the return of the 'primitive belief' of 'animism': finding soul or life in what you expected to be just a thing. Again, we find ourselves in the zone where animation and de-animation are intertwined as in Cholodenko's concept of 'the animatic', to which he therefore ascribes the quality of the Freudian uncanny.

The animated other

To Sianne Ngai, '[a]nimatedness seems to function as a marker of racial or ethnic otherness in general' (Ngai 2005: 94). Ngai shows how this mechanism is already at work in abolitionist literature, such as *Uncle Tom's Cabin*, when the praying Uncle Tom is described as 'enriched with the language of Scripture, which seemed to [...] drop from his lips unconsciously' (97). Tom is here animated, ventriloquized by the language of the Scripture. Emotional qualities slide into corporeal qualities, showing 'race as a truth in the [...] body' (95). In this process the body seems to be chopped up into its parts, which in Ngai's reasoning prefigures the way the cartoon figure is broken down into discrete parts in the Fordist production method of 2D celluloid animation, in which the character's body parts are posed and shifted on a celluloid layer placed on top of another layer with the trunk of the body (110).

The chopping up of the body into its parts, characteristic of earlier animation techniques, is still to be found in early Pixar productions. At the time of the very first Pixar short film, *The Adventures of André and Wally B* (Alvy Ray Smith, 1984), the modelling system could only handle geometrical shapes (spheres, cylinders, cones and so on), so the figures, the Android André and the bee Wally (named after the characters in Louis Malle's *My Dinner with André*), had to be put together by such parts. They could hardly be said, though, to be marked as racial or ethnic others.

But the kind of animatedness that Ngai describes, the chopped-up body marked by some kind of otherness, can be found in the potato characters from the *Toy Story* films. Their body parts are detachable, and notably Mrs Potato seems 'animated' in the excessive way that according to Ngai marks 'the other'. Generally, this kind of overexcited animatedness is in the Pixar films less to be found in the racial, ethnical other than in the sexual other, woman.

The guide: hysteric or pervert?

The analyses of Pixar's film in this book will examine how Pixar animates toys, animals, monsters, cars, fish, bugs and human figures by throwing them into the ban of the Other, giving them voice and gaze, inscribing them into the socio-symbolic order of desire and language, but also dealing with the automaton at the core of autonomy. Lacan will be a guide to Pixar when trying to understand animation not only as their technique, but also as their theme. And Pixar will be a guide to Lacan by (hopefully) giving us clear and imaginative images of 'the alien controlling our animal bodies', be it the rat under the toque or the electronic collar around the dog's neck.

But why 'The Hysteric's Guide'? This subtitle is first of all my homage to two great sources of inspiration: Juliet Flower MacCannell's book *The Hysteric's Guide to the Future Female Subject* (2000) and Sophie Fiennes' documentary featuring Slavoj Žižek: *The Pervert's Guide to Cinema* (2006).

According to Žižek, film is in itself a perverted art, because it makes the fantasy come true (or at least come 'alive' on the screen). Whereas the hysteric is the one who is driven by some partly or totally unconscious fantasy, which functions as a drive as long as it does not come true, the pervert is the one who acts out the fantasy. Whereas the hysteric is the one who doubts what she desires and is never satisfied, the pervert knows what he desires, and is satisfied when he gets it.

In Sophie Fiennes' film it is actually not the guide (Žižek) who is the pervert, but cinematic art itself. The guide acts more like a compulsive neurotic, the one who constructs or adapts a system to control the potentially anxiety-provoking sensory bombardment to which cinema exposes him. Žižek's system is the terms of philosophy and psychoanalysis, primarily Jacques Lacan.

But what about the hysteric? How could she be a guide? This is the question Juliet Flower MacCannell asks in *The Hysteric's Guide to the Future Female Subject*. MacCannell presents the pervert as the one who goes for unrestricted enjoyment, disavowing symbolic castration and sexual difference, like the Marquis de Sade. Whereas the pervert is sceptical regarding the law, the hysteric may be said to be hesitating before the law, like she hesitates before sexual difference: 'Am I a man or a woman?' (MacCannell 2000: 18). The hysteric is dominated by the superego that MacCannell with Klein calls sadistic: the one that has its image in the capricious mother rather than the lawful father. Her hesitation before the law goes with a longing for something beyond the law, something 'different' from the social order and dull life as she knows it. All this makes her attracted to the pervert: he promises an enjoyment 'beyond' law, dull life and sexual difference, he represents the sadism of her own superego. To MacCannell, the hysteric can be an important guide to understanding contemporary Western culture, in which the obscene part of the superego, which induces us to enjoy, seems to have become dominant.

MacCannell wishes for woman to find a solution other than the 'Sadean' one, that is to resist patriarchal law not by rejecting law and sexual difference altogether, but by finding her own way of entering the law, her own way of symbolic castration. Whereas Slavoj Žižek has become still more interested in the beyond the law, the real, MacCannell sticks more to the law, but discusses how it could be rethought, in order to contain the experience of 'the girl', so that the Sadean bed chamber is not her only alternative to the (patriarchal) law.

When I have presented my Pixar analyses in lectures under the title of 'The Hysteric's Guide', I have often been asked if they are really hysterical, as I do not seem to hesitate or doubt my findings or leave things open and mysterious. Rather, like Žižek, I make the images and stories fit perfectly together with the Lacanian terms. My spontaneous answer has been something like, 'Oh yes, perhaps you are right, I do not really know if my position is really hysterical' – which might at least be said to be a somewhat hysterical answer. Also, the hysteric is the one who cannot stop interpreting, like Paul Verhaeghe writes in his wonderful *Does the Woman Exist? From Freud's Hysteric to Lacan's Feminine* (1999): 'the best analysts are actually the hysterics themselves. If the analyst behind the couch produces one interpretation, the hysteric will add ten' (118). To Verhaeghe, this is because the hysteric does not really want to accept that Woman does not exist and produces all kinds of thoughts and images to cover up for this non-existent Woman. This makes her 'perfectly at home in the interpretative system' (118).

If there is something hysterical about my project, it may be my excessive desire to interpret. But also my partial desire to be 'one of the boys'. The universe of Pixar is something I have been sharing with my two sons since they were small. From the commentary tracks I have had a glimpse into the Pixar boys at their 'gag sessions', having hilarious fun while inventing incredible things. To be part of such a boys' team is definitely one of my fantasies.

In *The Pervert's Guide to Cinema* Žižek lets Lacan shed light on famous film scenes, and vice versa. This book's ambition is twofold in a similar way: I wish to analyse Pixar's oeuvre through Lacan, but I also wish to introduce the reader to Lacan's complicated writings and sayings through Pixar's relatively simple images and stories. Thus, each Pixar film becomes in this book an occasion to introduce yet another psychoanalytic idea or cluster of ideas. Chapter 1 analyses *Toy Story* focusing on voice and the symbolic versus the primal father, while Chapter 2 discusses gaze in *Toy Story 2*, including the split between the eye and the gaze and the turn from the imaginary look to the real gaze. The analysis of *Toy Story 3* in Chapter 3 focuses on the partial object, while *A Bug's Life* (Chapter 4) becomes the occasion for explaining the importance of language, signifiers and puns, in psychoanalysis. Chapter 5 introduces Lacan's four discourses through an analysis of *Monsters, Inc.* (including the sequel *Monsters University*), while Chapter 6 finds the death drive and the three orders (symbolic/imaginary/real) represented in the streams and zones of the sea in *Finding Nemo. The Incredibles* is analysed in Chapter 7 exploring the superman's burden as the surplus (the 'in-you-more-than-yourself'), the analysis of *Cars* (Chapter 8) focuses on the sustainment of paternal desire, and the analysis of *Ratatouille* (Chapter 9) explores the *objet-petit-a* as something suspended between sublime and excremental. Lacan's gender theory, the formulas of sexuation, will be unfolded in the analysis of *Wall-E* (Chapter 10) discussing also the equation of the difference between the masculine and feminine positions with the difference between Law and Love. Finally, in Chapter 11, the theme of speaking dogs in *Up* will incite us to unfold the discussion of the animal/human divide central to animation as well as psychoanalysis. The book does not include what is, apart from sequels and prequels, the latest Pixar production, *Brave*, as this film seems to me to be more a part of the Disney tradition, presenting the Scottish redheaded free-spirited princess Merida as an up-to-date version of the Disney princess. (*Brave* also diverges by being directed by Mark Andrews and Brenda Chapman, who are not part of the gang that directed and co-directed the twelve first full-length Pixar films: John Lasseter, Andrew Stanton, Brad Bird, Lee Unkrich and Pete Docter.)

The Pixar films abound in references to live action films. If this book has a special focus on the references to Hitchcock, it is because they are a meeting point for Pixar and the neo-Lacanians, who find in Hitchcock images incarnating Lacanian ideas such as the obscene superego (the mummy in *Psycho*), the split between the eye and the gaze (*Vertigo*), the alliance between the hysteric and the pervert (*Shadow of a Doubt*). Žižek's analyses of *Psycho*, *Vertigo* and *The Birds* (Žižek 1991, 1992) and MacCannell's analysis of *Shadow of a Doubt* (MacCannell 2000) have been important inspirations for me, and this book might as well have been called *Everything You Never Wanted to Know about Lacan, and Certainly Would Not Ask Pixar*, alluding to the volume edited by Žižek: *Everything You Always Wanted to Know about Lacan, but Were Afraid to Ask Hitchcock* (Žižek 1992).

Throughout the analyses the book also wants to examine the ideological implications of the images of human existence given in the Pixar films, which belong to the most popular family films worldwide today. Our children's imaginary is to a large degree fed on Pixar's images, stories and phantasies. Thus we might be curious about what these images actually are, what kind of ideas they propagate about being human.

1

Beyond the Name of the Father: *Toy Story*

In the very first 'birth scene' of an animated Pixar character that you could watch on screen, the cowboy doll Woody becoming alive in *Toy Story*, 'animation' is staged as voice and gaze: Woody is changed from a toy to a live character the moment he speaks, and his painted empty eyes become the site of a gaze.

Now, as voice and gaze may seem the trademarks of 'humanity' and 'subjectivity', Lacan nevertheless puts them on the side of the object, regarding them as potential partial objects, objects to be desired, and to be feared. I shall in this chapter inquire into the 'animation' of Woody as well as his seemingly psychotic pal, the space toy Buzz Lightyear. My analysis of *Toy Story* will take its point of departure in the dimension of the voice, whereas the dimension of the gaze will be central for my analysis of *Toy Story 2* (Chapter 2).

The basic scene of the *Toy Story* films is a boy's (Andy's) room, and the characters are his toys, coming alive whenever they are left on their own. The main characters are the cowboy doll Woody and the space toy Buzz Lightyear.

In *Toy Story* (John Lasseter, 1995) Buzz Lightyear (Tim Allen) arrives as Andy's birthday present and right away becomes his favourite toy, thus dethroning Woody (Tom Hanks). In a series of events initiated by Woody's jealousy, and by a detour to the fast food restaurant 'Pizza Planet', they both end up with the neighbour's boy Sid, who is a really bad kid, treating his toys sadistically, blowing them up or tearing them apart, putting them together again in surrealist constellations (like a doll's head with spider legs). In Sid's home, in a strangely touching scene, Buzz gets to realize through a TV commercial that he is not really a space ranger, but a mass-produced toy – thus he is not unique, and he cannot fly. Through cunning planning and by the help of Sid's surrealist creations, his kind of mutant toys, Woody and Buzz manage to scare Sid and escape from him, just as he is about to fire off Buzz, being bound to a big rocket, which becomes instead a means for Buzz and Woody to fire themselves into Andy's car, as he is moving with his mother to a new house. The moral seems quite clear: by overcoming your jealous rivalry, realizing your own limitations, and working together, you can make it. In its pedagogical address to children the film definitely deals with the problem of sibling rivalry. (As my younger son said, when he was seven years old: it is about being the super-coolest, and then somebody else arrives and becomes the super-coolest.)

The voice, the alien

In *The Pervert's Guide to Cinema*, Slavoj Žižek claims that cartoons as well as silent movies present us with a universe without guilt, sexuality and death, as those themes enter into human life only with the voice. In a lucid analysis of Chaplin's *The Great Dictator*, which has moments of silent as well as talking movie, he claims that this film is all about the problem of 'domesticating the terrifying dimension of the voice'. As long as Chaplin is the Jewish barber living in the peaceful ghetto, he is in the infantile universe of silent movie, with all its primitive laughs and aggressions and gags – as soon as he gets into the role of his double, the German dictator Hynkel, he is inhabited by a voice threatening to demonize him. In the final scene, when the Jewish barber dressed up as dictator gives his heroic speech promoting democratic values, Žižek remarks that his appearance and the enthusiastic reaction of the crowd do not differ very much from the situation of the totalitarian dictator. Even if Chaplin here preaches nice, democratic values, the very demon of the voice has entered his body, threatening to transform him into just a copy of the dictator he is verbally attacking. Thus the voice becomes an instance of that 'alien' which, according to Žižek (and psychoanalysis in general) is at the core of humanity: 'Humanity means: the alien is controlling our animal bodies' (Žižek in Fiennes 2006, *The Pervert's Guide to Cinema*).

When we look at the history of animated film, it surely takes its beginning as silent movie, in that 'anal-oral-egoistic' universe which Žižek finds ruling those innumerable cartoons where animated animals are chasing and mutilating each other – and which might actually seem a perfect illustration of the paranoid-schizoid universe of the infant as Melanie Klein describes it: the universe where there is nothing between one being and another but revengeful aggression and attacks. Actually, animated film is still often silent movie, and the truth about voice even in live action (that it is not emitted from the body images on the screen, but from another source) is more evident in animated talkies. In the animated universe of Pixar the voice is certainly one of the constitutive features of 'animation' in the sense of bringing human life into the representations of things and animals.

Turning to Woody's 'birth scene' in *Toy Story*, we may start by observing that he actually has two 'birth scenes' in the film, two crucial moments of becoming alive. The first one is in the film's first scene when Woody is left on the bed by Andy, having until then been the one to 'animate' him as the child animates his toy. The second one is towards the end of the film, scene 26, when Woody is placed on the barbecue by the sadistic neighbour kid Sid, but starts pronouncing threats with his mechanical voice and finally 'comes alive' in Sid's hand, talking to him, and staring directly at him. Whereas the gaze and the voice in the first scene humanize Woody, in the scene at Sid's they rather demonize him. When traumatized Sid tells his sister, 'the toy is alive', this is (at it would be in reality) really, really scary.

So what animates us, what inhabits us? Is it a soul, or is it a demon? Do the voice and the gaze stem from some kind of inner source of humanity – or are they rather transplanted into our bodies? In the case of animation movies, the voice is clearly something that is put into the figure (and sometimes actually changes the character, as becomes clear from the commentary track to *Toy Story*, where the animators tell us that Tim Allen's voice made them change Buzz from a superhero to a space cop). In *Toy Story*, furthermore, both Buzz and Woody have both a mechanical and a human voice, and what happens in Woody's animation at Sid's is a kind of fusion of those two: Woody is talking with his mechanical voice, but he is free to say what he wants, not just replay the same mechanical and rather idiotic sentence ('there is a snake in my boot').

Departing from Žižek's point: 'Humanity means: the alien is controlling our human bodies', Woody's second animation scene is perhaps not contradictory to his first, but rather its truth: humanization is just as much a demonization, a being invaded by the alien, the voice. Thus the 'animation' of the animated film might be seen as a familiarization of something which is actually deeply unfamiliar and scary.

Falling with style

The story of Buzz Lightyear's fall, central to *Toy Story*, is yet another story of what animates the subject. The fall may be seen as constituting Buzz as a neurotic. Until then his character matches Lacan's definition of the psychotic: the one who firmly believes in the big Other.

As explained in the introduction to this book, the big Other (French: *L'Autre*) is Lacan's concept for that place – be it a person, an ideology, God, common sense – where I believe the truth about my existence, the meaning of my life, the guarantee of my identity, to be located. For Buzz Lightyear, the big O is the outer space control from which he (thoroughly psychotically) believes he has been sent on a mission.

In *Toy Story*, in the scenes taking place in the fast food restaurant 'Pizza Planet', one may observe yet another allegory for big O: 'the claw'. The claw is placed in an automate where children can catch small, green, plastic Martians. As Woody and Buzz fall down in the automate, we experience 'the Claw' from the small Martians' perspective – and here it certainly functions as 'the big O': the God-like instance 'choosing' certain of its creatures to be lifted. In the DVD version of *Toy Story*, the menu is designed as a TV screen being watched by the small, green Martians, waiting excitedly for the choice of the remote control. Thus the position of the spectator is given as the position of a small plastic Martian, and the TV screen becomes the place from which the big Other emanates. This is something recurrent in Pixar: it is by watching a screen that the characters come to know their desire. This may be both the wish of a movie company, and a truth of our time: the screen is what animates us.

Back to Buzz: his confrontation with the screen is actually something other than the affirmation of imaginary identity, on the contrary it is the deconstruction of imaginary identity – the moment when he is forced to give up his firm belief in the big O. It is spelt out on the screen that he is just one in a series, 'not a flying toy', and that he is 'made in Taiwan', which is confirmed when Buzz, horrified, observes that writing on his wing. Thus Buzz could be said to be awakening from his psychotic delusion: the subject discovers that he is not an instrument of some all-knowing big Other, he is just a product in a multiple series of similar products, and he does not have any supernatural powers. It is the moment when he realizes what Woody has been screaming to him earlier in the film: 'YOU ARE A TOY'.

To put it in another way, Buzz realizes that he is not *the* Buzz Lightyear, he is just *a* Buzz Lightyear. This is how Woody puts it in a scene before the fall when he says reproachfully: 'You really think you are *the* Buzz Lightyear?', and then there is a scene after the fall when he says approvingly and encouragingly: 'You're *a* Buzz Lightyear' (which is a very fine thing to be). One might say that here Woody behaves as a really bad shrink, telling Buzz a truth he is not yet ready to face. Furthermore, in his remark 'You are not the real Buzz Lightyear' Woody seems himself to be deluded, as if 'the real Buzz Lightyear' (and not just copies) existed. Altogether one cannot blame Buzz for answering, when Woody screams into his head: 'YOU-ARE-A-TOY', 'You are a little sad man, and you have my pity.'

Now, Buzz's condition is not just some 'toyish' condition, but rather an allegory of the human condition: the big Other and our imaginary identity are illusions, and somehow we have to realize that, painful as it may be.

The moment when Buzz gives up the idea of some unique, essential identity is the moment when he becomes the subject of his own desire, his own mission (instead of this mission of the big O from outer space). Even if one must of course be strictly aware that he is on a mission for Pixar, whatever kind of big O that might be . . .

Buzz's fall is clearly staged as castration, a feminization: he loses his arm, and after the fall Sid's sister dresses him up as 'Mrs Nesbit' in apron and hat, and places him at a doll's tea table where he gets drunk on Darjeeling: 'The one minute I am defending the whole galaxy, the next minute I am sucking down Darjeeling.'

Furthermore the fall is staged as a crucifixion (after the fall Buzz forms a cross on the floor), which makes of Woody a Judas, who is according to Žižek the greatest ethical hero of the Bible, being the traitor whose act is necessary for Jesus/Buzz to fulfil his mission.

What Buzz is going through is what Lacanian psychoanalysis calls a subjective destitution: the subject realizing, as Žižek puts it in his colloquial way, that it is

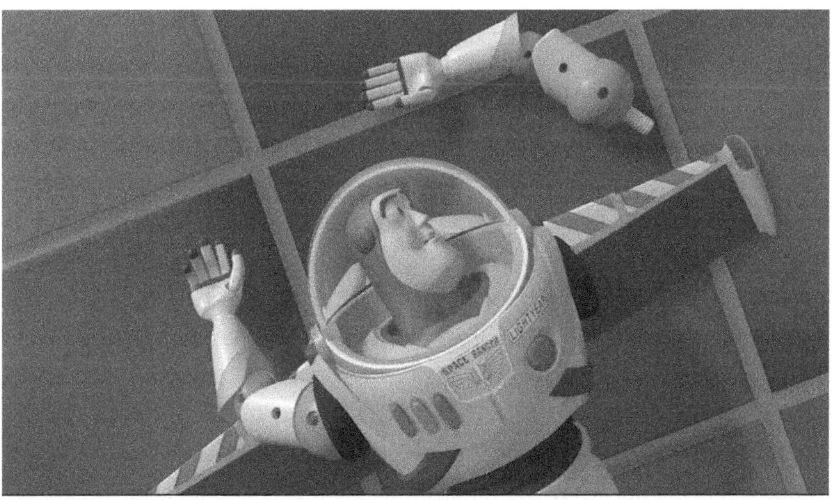

Figure 1 Buzz Lightyear forming a cross. From *Toy Story* (John Lasseter, 1995) © Pixar.

just a piece of shit, thereby actually and paradoxically gaining its subjectivity. When you give up the illusion of your subjectivity as a unique kernel, you gain your subjectivity as that which it really is: a knot in a network, the crossing of several inscriptions: 'Made in Taiwan', 'Walt Disney Productions' (stamped on Buzz's behind, shown in a very quick glimpse when he is falling), 'Andy' (Andy writes his name on his toys' soles, including Buzz's).

When you realize that you cannot fly, you are able to fall with style (which is Woody's wording, finally taken over by Buzz: 'I am not flying, I am falling with style').

Beyond the name-of-the-father

Toy Story seems at first sight to represent a universe where fathers are absent. It is as if Andy only has a mother, even if there is no allusion to divorce or father's death. Sid's father is only represented by an arm, sticking out from the back of an armchair in front of the TV, whereas his mother, if not visually appearing, is at least represented by an articulated voice. But actually Andy and Sid could be seen themselves as father figures, as they are a kind of fathers to their toys.

From a Lacanian perspective, Andy represents the symbolic father, also known as the-name-of-the-father. This is the father as the function of inscribing the child into social order. Andy's name very explicitly has this function of giving social identity to his toys: he marks them by writing his name on their soles. What saves Buzz from insanity is actually this very name-of-the-father written on his sole – when he sees it he gets out of his post-castration depression and takes action. So when it comes to the question of what makes a subject a subject, the film also points to this social inscription, the name-of-the-father. Buzz has more than one name-of-the-father, more than one social inscription: 'Andy' is supplemented by 'Made in Taiwan' and 'Walt Disney Productions' (which may also be seen as Pixar's ironic tribute to their name-of-the-father). The subject is a product; humanity is a trade mark. Thus the film points to the fact that we are socially always products of more than one 'father'; the inscriptions quilting us to the social world are not only our family name, but also names of other social forces than that of the family.

The series of such 'brands' or 'inscriptions' or 'castration marks' in the film is extensive: besides the literal inscriptions you have Buzz losing his arm, and Woody having a mark burned into his front like a kind of Kain's mark (one may observe how this mark is prefigured by Buzz directing his impotent laser ray against Woody, and then inscribed for real when Sid burns a mark in Woody's front by capturing rays of the sun in a looking glass). The Kain's mark may allude to the theme of sibling rivalry, which is certainly an important theme in the Buzz/Woody relationship, but at the same time it marks that symbolic castration which has to happen to Woody as well, in order for the two of them to be able to 'share the fall' – which might be one way of defining love, and which is very literally what happens in the final scene when together they are 'falling with style' into Andy's car.

Compared with Andy as the symbolic father, Sid could be said to represent the primal father, the one that tends to take over in the symbolic father's absence, as Paul Verhaeghe makes clear in his article 'The Collapse of the Function of the Father and its Effects on Gender Roles': 'Instead of the real primal father, it is the symbolic function which is destroyed, thereby setting loose what Lacan calls the primal anal father, a figure who is only on the lookout for his own *jouissance*' (Verhaeghe 2000: 138). Sid bears the marks of this 'father-of-enjoyment' (Lacan: *père-jouisseur*): his sadistic behaviour, his satanic laughter, his passion for the fantasmatic phallus (the rocket called 'the big One' to which he attaches Buzz), his bad teeth that tend to be a characteristic of the visualizing of this fantasmatic figure (think of Bobby Peru/Willem Dafoe in David Lynch's *Wild at Heart*).

In this seemingly fatherless universe, Andy and Sid thus may be seen as allegories of the symbolic versus the primal father. The film shows us how the name of the father can save us from psychosis (as it saves Buzz), and how its disappearance gives way to the sadistic primal father of enjoyment.

One interesting aspect of the character of Sid, though, is the creativeness of his sadistic operations. When you listen to the commentary track you will hear the animators saying that they identify with Sid, and not with Andy. Andy is the strange guy, treating his toys neatly and nicely, whereas blowing up G.I. Joes and tearing apart mechanical toys is what the animators remember themselves doing as kids. And Sid's creations surely look like surrealist pieces of art. In their final coming together against Sid his mutant creations become a kind of zombies, turning themselves against the force that has distorted their very being, thus representing a kind of rebellious potentiality in the very products of the destructive force (something like the replicants in Scott Ridley's *Blade Runner*). In his sadistic way of treating the toys Sid may even be representing that 'metaphysical tendency' that Baudelaire sees in children tearing their toys apart in order to find their souls: 'at last he opens it up, he is the stronger, But *where is the soul?* This is the beginning of melancholy and gloom [l'hébétement et la tristesse]' (Baudelaire 1853).

Kiss my butt

Mutilation occurs in three different versions in *Toy Story*.

First we have that anal-oral mutilation that Žižek rightly sees as characteristic of cartoons, in the figure of 'Mr Potato Head', whose partial objects (eyes, mouth, feet, arms, ears) are all de- and re-attachable, as they would be in a universe before symbolic castration, before finitude and mortality. In the beginning the figure is used very literally in an anal-oral joke, taking off his mouth and holding it to his behind, thus incarnating the verbal expression: 'kiss my butt' – a joke that the film-makers really enjoyed as is clear from their commentary track. The orality is furthermore stressed as Andy's little sister takes Mr Potato in her mouth, biting off several parts that he will afterwards have to re-collect while complaining about 'Princess Drool'.

Secondly we have the phallic mutilation, the castration represented by Buzz's loss of his arm. A loss that might be seen as compensated through the big fantasmatic phallus that is tied to his back in the form of Sid's rocket – a phallus that it takes some cunning, though, for Buzz not to become its victim, but its master.

Besides this anal-oral and phallic mutilation we thirdly have Sid's mutilation of his toys, which may on the one hand be seen as the cruel (sadistic) version of anal-orality ('Princess Drool' being the innocent version), while on the other hand as a creative process in which dismembered entities are put together in new constellations. Sid's creations might be seen as a result of that switching between the paranoid-schizoid (mutilating) and the depressive (recreating) positions that is to Melanie Klein a condition of the subject in general – and of creativity in particular. (The sadistic component of play and creativity shall be further explored in the analysis of *Toy Story 3*, Chapter 3.)

The difference between anal-oral and phallic mutilation is correlative to the difference between different kinds of partial objects, or perhaps rather between partial objects and the phallus, between Mr Potato's parts and Sid's rocket 'the big One'. In between we would have Buzz's arm, lingering between being (as a metaphor) the sign of symbolic castration and (as a metonym) the sign of sadistic mutilation.

The fall of Buzz is one in a series of falls throughout the film. First we have Woody falling down on the floor (as an expression of his being dethroned by Buzz). Then we have Buzz 'flying' in Andy's room in a scene in which the surroundings provide him with what Lacan would call an 'answer of the real'

(Žižek 1991: 29–30): the things by accident catching and throwing him, thus supporting his imaginary belief, making of his fall what looks like flying. After Buzz's big fall we then finally have the common fall of Buzz and Woody into the car. Here our heroes succeed in not just being victims of the unavoidable 'fall', but sharing it and directing it to match their desire (returning to Andy). This may be what 'falling with style' is about. The motto of Buzz Lightyear: 'To infinity and beyond' (meant by the film-makers to be a ridiculous hyperbole) is repeated by the two friends in the final fall, but the meaning seems transformed: 'beyond infinity' is no longer the fantasmatic superlative of a megalomaniac, but could rather be read as the expression that we are now beyond the illusion of the infinity of the subject; we are able to deal with mortality and fall as parts of the human condition.

As suggested answers to the question 'What animates us?' *Toy Story* has given us the voice, the gaze, the name-of-the-father, the fantasy of the father-of-enjoyment, the fall, the phallus . . . In the analysis of *Toy Story 2* we shall get more into the function of the gaze.

2

Big O is Watching You: *Toy Story 2*

To psychoanalysis the subject is constituted by a lack, a split, a fissure. We may have dreams of being complete, and perhaps at a very early, infantile or even embryonic stage of our lives we felt no lack, no split, no separation, being just one with whatever surrounded us. But as far as we are creatures of language and desire (and to Lacan language and desire are what separates the human from the animal being), we are split beings: split between the thing and the word for it, between what we want and what we get, between what we feel like and what we look like, between present and past, between what we think we say or want and what we actually say or want, between conscious and unconscious. Being split from temporality: the impossibility of a complete present moment, uncontaminated by past or future, from desire: the impossibility of complete and permanent satisfaction, from mortality: the horizon of 'nothingness' surrounding our existence.

In his seminar XI, in the lecture called *Le schism de l'oeuil et du regard* ('The Split between the Eye and the Gaze'), Lacan stages the fissure of the subject as the fissure of the eye, being both the site of looking and a thing, an object, a partial object. Like when you think of your own eyes as on one hand the hole, the nothing in your face from where you see the world (but not your own face) – and on the other hand as material eyeballs. Lacan puts the gaze on the side of the object, stating it as the object of the scopic drive: 'The *object a* in the field of the visible is the gaze' (Lacan 1979: 105). What on earth does that mean? On the one hand it means that our eyeballs desire to be filled with the gaze, to become the site of looking instead of just empty globes. On the other hand it means that what we really desire to see (for instance when at a cinema) is the gaze of the Other. Now, the Other, or big O, is this fantasmatic instance ('the subject-supposed-to-know') to whom and for whose approval we are, consciously or not, performing the comedy of our lives – be it our mother, our God, lifestyle magazines or something more abstract. We desire this gaze to rest upon us, and we desire to meet it. But when this seems to actually happen, it can be a most creepy experience. As Žižek argues in *Everything You Always Wanted to Know about Hitchcock, but Were Afraid to Ask Lacan*, finally looking into the gaze of big O would be something like looking into the gaze of Norman Bates in the final scene of *Psycho* (a scene in which both voice and gaze surely seem as 'aliens' animating a human body) (Žižek 1992: 245).

The gaze of the skull

Lacan's most famous example to explain the turning point where the desired and idealized gaze of the big O turns out to be a scary, annihilating gaze of the big Zero, is Hans Holbein's painting from 1533, 'The Ambassadors' (now in the National Gallery, London: http://www.nationalgallery.org.uk/paintings/hans-holbein-the-younger-the-ambassadors). In this painting you see two richly dressed ambassadors posing, leaning on a table where their books and instruments, signs of their mastering the world, are exposed. In the foreground some strange amorphous white-greyish spot is lingering.

Now, those two men could be said to be posing as imaginary personae for the gaze of the big O – which is what we always do when we are being painted, or (today, more likely and much more common) photographed. The gaze here being the public gaze, to which they are showing themselves off – at that time represented by the artist's gaze, as it would be today by the camera. But there is another, creepy gaze present in the painting: if you get to look at the spot in the foreground from the right (oblique) angle, you will see that it is actually – a skull. The spectator's desire for the gaze (reflecting the ambassadors' desire for the gaze of the imaginary big O) will be mockingly satisfied by the anamorphically distorted skull, the very symbol of vanity. If we really get to see the gaze, it will be the gaze of the real, looking back at us with no other message than the message of the mortality of the subject. (It should be noticed that the subject, the artist, has inscribed his mortal name in the skull, which could thus be seen as a kind of signature: 'Holbein' meaning 'hollow bone'.)

Thus the painting makes us experience the difference between the gaze in 'the imaginary' and the gaze in 'the real', those concepts being understood as two of the three Lacanian orders, the third being 'the symbolic'. The symbolic order is, in Lacan's definition, the social and verbal world into which we are born; in the symbolic the subject is the subject of language, desire and social order, being marked by that split or lack or fissure (called 'the symbolic castration') implied in speaking, desiring and being a social creature. In the imaginary the subject is without this fissure: complete (as we can dream to be 'whole' and 'perfect' figures, be it in a new age dream of being present, or in a teenage dream of becoming a star). In the real the subject is that which escapes symbolic (verbal, social) definition as well as imaginary ideals: mortal body and ungraspable spectrality.

So in the imaginary the subject is 'something', in the real he is 'nothing' – and in the symbolic, if he subjects himself to it without making of his symbolic position (be it 'man' or 'professor' or 'space ranger') an imaginary identification, he is 'not nothing'. As in the example of Buzz Lightyear: believing he is really 'something' (*the* Buzz Lightyear on a mission from the big O, aka outer space), coming through his fall to find himself as 'nothing', and finally realizing that he is 'not nothing' (*a* Buzz Lightyear).

The two dimensions of the gaze of the Other have been termed by Todd McGowan 'the imaginary look' (the camera before which you are posing) and 'the real gaze' (the skull suddenly staring back at you) (McGowan 2007: 1). McGowan renews Lacanian film theory by turning the focus from 'the imaginary look' (film as ideal images dictated by the dominating ideology, including ideal images of women dictated by patriarchy) to 'the real gaze' (cinema as the place where you can actually meet Norman Bates staring back at you).

Woody caught by his image

There is a scene in *Toy Story 2* in which the dialectics of the gaze is performed at aesthetic and philosophical height with Hans Holbein: the scene where 'the cleaner' comes to repair Woody. Before turning to this scene, though, a short summary of the film's plot is needed.

In *Toy Story 2* (John Lasseter, Ash Brannon, Lee Unkrich, 1999) Woody (Tom Hanks) learns about vanity. Both in the sense of being obsessed with one's own image, and in the sense of mortality. As Johannes Wende has remarked, vanity and mortality are the recurring themes of the *Toy Story* films, even if no longer (as in photographic films) in accordance with the medium; computer-animated films do not capture a fugitive moment, and their 'physical body' is 'any time replaceable' (Wende 2014: 61). In the beginning of the film, while Andy is playing with him, his arm loosens. As a result he is not coming with Andy to 'cowboy camp', but put on the shelf (the toys have a word for this: 'being shelved') where he finds 'Squeezy', an old dust-covered plastic penguin whose 'squeeze' does not work any more and who has a psychedelic nightmare (not unlike the nightmare sequel from Hitchcock's *Vertigo*) about Andy throwing him into the dustbin in a whirling fall among loose parts of broken toys. Next day, Squeezy is collected by Andy's mother for a yard sale; in saving him Woody ends up as an item in the sale himself. He is spotted by the fat and greedy toy collector Al (Wayne Knight) who finally steals him as Andy's mother does not want to sell him. In the collector's home Woody finds out that he is star of a former TV show for kids and part of a toy 'set', including the cowgirl Jessie (Joan Cusack), the prospector Stinky Pete (Kelsey Grammer) and the horse Bullseye. He meets the other figures from his set and falls completely in love with his own appearance on the TV screen. Trying to escape, though, his loose arm falls completely off, but in the most fascinating scene in the film he is repaired by an old toy specialist called 'the cleaner', and finally is ready to be sent by aeroplane to the museum in Tokyo that has bought the whole set of cowboy toys expensively. Andy's other toys, though, have set out to rescue him, finding their way to 'Al's Toy Barn', where a hilarious comedy of exchange is played out between Buzz Lightyear (Tim Allen) and his (still deluded) double: one of the numerous other 'Buzzes' on the shelf getting out of his box, for a time replacing the 'real' Buzz, but finally being discovered and left behind in happy harmony with his former enemy and most Darth Vaderish father, Zurg (having declared himself with the *Star Wars* line: 'I am your father'). After a thrilling hunt at the airport, where Woody's arm falls off again, the toys, including the rest of Woody's set, are all back in Andy's home – and Andy sews Woody's arm back on in clumsy boy's stitches, as a counterpoint to the perfect reparation by 'the cleaner'.

There are several similarities between the plots and themes of *Toy Story* and *Toy Story 2*: a toy is taken away from home by some evil force, be it the neighbour's kid or the toy collector, experiencing some kind of symbolic castration or even crucifixion. (Buzz and Woody both loose one arm, Buzz as he tries to fly, and Woody as he tries to escape – and after their dismembrance they are both staged in a kind of 'imitatio Christi': Buzz lying as a cross on the floor, Woody hanging on his metal cross in the collector's glass box.) But whereas Buzz's symbolic castration takes him out of his psychotic delusion that he is on a mission from outer space (an instrument of some big Other), Woody's castration (which has to happen twice) finally takes him out of his narcissist infatuation with his own appearance (his imaginary posing before the big Other).

The eye as a stain

Addressing the theme of vanity and the gaze, let us start with the scene where 'the cleaner' (Jonathan Harris) comes to fix Woody's arm – to me one of the best scenes in Pixar ever. Through the technique of montage the scene subtly stages the play between the eye as the site of gaze and as an object, *le schism de l'oeuil et du regard*, as Lacan calls it. The music for the scene is reminiscent of Tchaikovsky's *The Nut Cracker*, or Offenbach's *The Tales of Hoffmann*, and thus suggests the theme of toys becoming alive, like the toys in E. T. A. Hoffmann's tales, not least the doll Olimpia in 'Der Sandmann' in which the gaze and the loose eyeball play an important part.

As the old 'cleaner' (an allusion to Harvey Keitel's character in *Pulp Fiction*), with his big nose and his white, hairy eyebrows, is approaching Woody, the point of view is switching between the cleaner and Woody, whose eyes in the 'objective' shot of his face are just painted surfaces, no site of the gaze. Well seated vis-à-vis Woody, placing his toolbox on the table and Woody in a metal clamp like in a barber's or dentist's chair, the old man takes out an optic glass to have a closer look at his 'specimen'. This glass becomes to the spectator a screen through which the cleaner's eye is looking, as well as the screen through which we are looking at the cleaner's eye. Thus we are switching between the eye as the site of the gaze, and the eye as the object to be gazed upon. Furthermore, the eye as an object is represented in this scene by the loose eyeballs in the cleaner's toolbox.

Another tool besides the looking glass functions as an axis between the old man and Woody, between eye-as-subject and eye-as-object, and that is the cotton pin with which the old man cleans Woody's eye. We see the pin approaching from Woody's point of view – and then we actually share his experience of getting it into the eye: the cotton of the pin fills out the whole screen which then for a moment goes completely white, cutting to the scene in the toy store which breaks up the cleaner scene as an intermezzo. This 'white out' is later repeated in a 'black out' when we, for a moment, in a really crazy shot, seem to experience the situation from the gap in Woody's body, closing as the old man is sewing the arm back on.

The scene's switching between subjective and objective shot may remind us of that which Žižek calls the 'Hitchcockian montage' (for instance the switch in *Psycho* between Lilah looking at Norman's gothic house, and some indiscernible point in the house looking back at her) (Žižek 1991: 117). This kind of montage implies the experience of the object looking back, which might be said to be the general idea of the *Toy Story* films: the toy is looking back; the world is seen from the toy's perspective.

Figure 2 The impossible shot from Woody's armpit. From *Toy Story 2* (John Lasseter, 1999) © Pixar.

The cleaner scene in *Toy Story 2* actually is montage to a higher degree than any other Pixar scene – it is more cut than any other scene (that is what we are told in the commentary track). At the same time one must notice that the camera in this scene is moving in a smooth and sliding, almost caressing way, in this way kind of harmonizing the cut, the fissure, the schism between the eye and the gaze, just as the cleaner is actually repairing Woody.

Despite the smoothing, harmonizing camera, one might argue, though, that in this scene we get close to the real gaze – which appears as a stain in our visual field. The stain representing the real of the gaze is for instance the skull in Holbein's painting, or the birds in Hitchcock's *The Birds*. In the cleaner scene the stain might be said to be represented by Woody's blind, painted, wooden eyes, or by that black out which appears when in a split second the point of view moves to this really crazy, impossible place: the fibres of the cloth of Woody's shirt, closing as the old man is sewing.

Nostalgia and montage

The main theme of *Toy Story 2* may be seen as Woody's lingering between being exposed to 'the real gaze', and to 'the imaginary look'. Exposed to the real gaze he becomes the object of mortality; exposed to the imaginary look, watching himself as a TV star, he becomes the object of the big Other as in the mirror stage. The scene when he is watching himself starring in the TV show 'Woody's Roundup' is wonderful: his face and his whole body irradiates infatuation – this is how a man looks when he falls completely in love with his own image.

The play between real gaze and imaginary look in the film stages the story of Woody's objectification, showing itself in the real (as Woody becoming a dead or mortal body), in the symbolic (Woody becoming a commodity, an object of exchange), and in the imaginary (the fantasmatic side of the commodity; Woody as a precious collector's item). In his Marxist analysis of Woody as commodity (in the film, but also as Pixar merchandise), Alan Ackerman reminds us of Walter Benjamin's definition of 'aura' as the ability of the inanimate object to return the human gaze (Ackerman 2011: 101, Benjamin 1968: 220–2). Woody has this 'aura', and the repair scene to Ackerman represents 'the wonder of art as much as that of resurrection' (Ackerman 2011: 110). Ackerman also interprets Al's project to move the toys from historical time to the sphere of art (selling them to the museum in Tokyo) as a redemptive project.

Toy Story 2 even seems to play out an allusion to that Hitchcock film in which the gaze is the most predominant theme: *Vertigo*. The psychedelic style of Woody's dream in the beginning of the film is reminiscent of James Stewart's nightmare in *Vertigo*, and Woody's whirling and seemingly endless fall into the abyss of the dustbin is a version of that fall into the swirl of the abyss that *Vertigo* is all about, and that might convincingly be interpreted as the fall into the abyss of the human eye (Žižek 1991: 87). With Woody also a set of playing cards fall to the floor, uncannily revealing themselves to be all aces of spades, all looking like black pupillaries on the white background of the playing cards. (According to the commentary track, the ace of spades was chosen because in Tarok it is the card of death, but this extra-filmic allegorical meaning does not annul the intra-filmic visual suggestion of pupillaries, contributing to the theme of the gaze.) Thus, Woody's anxious experience of mortality is coupled to images that might be interpreted as the experience of the eye as a flat surface or an abyss rather than a site of the look and a mirror of the soul.

According to Žižek in *Looking Awry*, there are three filmic ways to cope with 'the gaze', or with the antinomy between the eye and the gaze: pornography, nostalgia and finally montage (Žižek 1991: 107). In pornography the spectator is paralysed by being reduced to the object-gaze, which is thus absent from the picture. (Please notice that this is quite another way of understanding pornography than the way of Laura Mulvey (1975). Mulvey regards the position of the spectator as that of the subject-master – with Žižek he is rather the object-victim.) In nostalgia the gaze of the Other is included as the innocent and naive gaze that supports the gaze of the spectator: we imagine a gaze to which the world portrayed is completely natural and familiar. Montage, finally, is the most faithful to the antinomy between eye and gaze.

In his interesting conjunction of Spielberg and Disney, Rex Butler focuses on the link between nostalgia and animation. He points to the moment in *Schindler's List* when a small girl, hand-coloured in red, as an instance of animation, appears in the otherwise black-and-white film. It is in the middle of the massacre in the Cracow ghetto. Schindler watches it from above and suddenly sees this small girl, who looks back at him. At the other moment of the film when the hand-coloured red figure of the small girl appears, she is on a cart-load of dead bodies in the concentration camp. Butler describes those moments as 'moments of primitive, child-like animation' and partly suggests the red girl to be a version of the Lacanian 'stain', partly to be that gaze of the child supporting the nostalgic gaze (Butler 2007: 321). Altogether Butler does not see the girl's gaze as the unsettling gaze of the Real disturbing the subject's imaginary identity, but rather as a fantasized answer of the Real confirming the subject's imaginary identity (Schindler as the Jews' saviour). Still, his interpretation seems to linger between the girl's gaze as the support of nostalgia and as the skull-like gaze of the real. The cartoon-like quality of the girl, her being hand-coloured in red, might even make her a kind of cover-up for the Lacanian skull. Following Žižek, Butler defines Spielberg's film as nostalgic because it is made for a look that is now missing. He identifies this look with 'the Jews who vanished in Holocaust' (321), but I think this needs a precision: the small girl represents the vanishing gaze of the innocent Jew, the Jew who does not yet know Holocaust; what vanishes in Holocaust before the Jews themselves is the innocent look. Butler even plays with the idea that after the moment of the red-coloured girl's gaze, the film can be seen as Schindler's fantasy, the story of his saving the Jews, structured by that very gaze.

Thus, Butler relates Spielberg's nostalgic mode to the mode of animation. The animated moments in *Schindler's List*, and the animist, uncanny universe of *E.T.*, 'in which spirits are real and the distinction between the living and the dead, the human and the alien, no longer holds' (322–3). Of interest to my analysis of the *Toy Story* films is his further relating nostalgia and animation to the absence of fathers. Seeing *E.T.* as Spielberg's attempt to go back to 'that moment when he was able to believe in cartoons' he relates the recurring absence of fathers in Spielberg's films to 'unsupervised childhood watching of TV': 'It is the absence of the Symbolic paternal law that allows that suspension of disbelief which is the Imaginary' (323). Following Butler, we might say that the absence of fathers in the *Toy Story* films, and in particular their recurring theme of the grown-up man sleeping in front of the TV, is supportive of their nostalgic mode. But perhaps more correctly the suspension of disbelief as the suspension of paternal law has two sides to it: a nostalgic one, making space for the imaginary, and a scarier one, making space for the real.

To put it in another way: if the suspension of paternal law is to result in nostalgia and not psychosis, it needs to be supported by a big Other in the guise of the 'subject supposed to believe', the gaze of the Jewish girl before Holocaust, E.T.'s gaze from the cupboard, or the fantasy of 'the child's gaze' in general as a fantasy animating the Pixar animators.

In *Toy Story*, and in Pixar's animation films in general, nostalgia may seem the most adequate description of the dominant visual mode. The films depend on what Žižek calls 'the subject supposed to believe' (Žižek 2006: 29), in this case the child, the fantasy of whom actually is what animates the animators. The 'subject supposed to believe' is a variation of 'the subject supposed to know'. We depose the innocent, naive, believing gaze in the eyeballs of the child, thus supporting our own enjoyment. Nevertheless, I have tried through the cleaner scene to show also an element of montage and of exposing the stain, the real gaze.

The virtual, the real

Turning to computer-animated films, as a Lacanian cultural analyst one must consider the question of whether virtual reality in itself somehow excludes the real. 'Virtual reality [...] provides reality itself divested of its substance, of the resisting hard kernel of the real' (Žižek 2006: 38), thereby joining the phenomena that Žižek has cleverly seen as characteristic of our late capitalist culture: matters being deprived of their dangerous substance, such as coffee without caffeine, beers without alcohol, sweets without sugar, vampires without (human) blood (as in *True Blood* and *Twilight*). So, when film is deprived of human bodies, is it deprived of the hard kernel of the real?

Here, perhaps, the one human presence of Pixar's animation films, the voice, being actually performed by live actors, comes to play a role. Even in other dimensions the computer-animated construction of reality (as opposed to 'the real') is actually not completely controlled: the medium will react in unforeseen ways, and the crossing of story, animation, music, lines, characters in combination with the amount of people working to create the film will make the result unpredictable.

Žižek relates virtual reality to what he calls interpassivity (as opposed to interactivity), and of which he sees Hollywood as an agent: Hollywood takes care of our feelings, so that we can just sit down in the cinema and relax. Žižek sees this as a modern, sentimental version of the chorus in Greek tragedies (Žižek 2006: 22). If one wants a Greek chorus in *Toy Story*, one should just turn on the commentary track. In one scene in *Toy Story 2*, when the cowgirl Jessie sings her very sad song about being abandoned by the child who once loved her, the commentary goes: 'It's so emotional, there is so much emotion in this scene – oh, the amount of emotion that she puts into this song.'

Woman between maniac and zombie

The cowgirl Jessie was, according to the commentary track, created as an answer to the demand for 'a strong female character'. This seems quite comical, or perhaps quite symptomatic of our time, as Jessie's 'strength', if she has any, is a kind of boyish wildness. When Jessie first appears, she actually seems to be a complete maniac: attacking Woody with her uninhibited enthusiasm, screaming: 'it's you, it's you, it's you'. Later on we learn that besides this maniac mood, Jessie can get really blue; she is provided with a 'traumatic' psychobiography, told in her sad song, 'When somebody loves you', about being a girl's greatest love, until that girl grew into a giggling teenager painting her nails and not playing with toys anymore. The 'flashback' scene in which Jessie for a moment believes that the grown-up Emily has finally taken her back – only to find that she is taking her to the dump – is highly sentimental.

Actually, with her switching between mania and the blues, Jessie inaugurates what seems to be a persistent type in Pixar: the manic-depressive female character, later to be found for instance in *Wall-E* and *Up*. In *Wall-E* we have the character of 'Eve', the Mac-like, white and aerodynamically shaped robot who either freaks out completely in Wall-E's garage, threatening to smash up everything in her wild dance, or, after having been fertilized, falls into a death-like slumber, closing upon herself. In *Up* we have Fredericksen's wife, being both the little completely uninhibited girl invading Fredericksen as a boy, and the grown-up woman folding herself together in her grief for the child she cannot have. This is clearly one picture of 'femininity' in Pixar: women are either uninhibited maniacs or depressive zombies. It corresponds to two typical 'feminine' positions in our culture: Woman as the one who cannot contain herself, who is somehow flowing over her borders, and Woman as the mystery closing upon herself in some kind of secret communion (Freud's 'dark continent', Lacan's feminine position).

Gaining from loss

When Woody chooses to stay with his 'set' and be sent to the museum in Tokyo, he chooses to stay in the projector of the imaginary look, being its precious object. The smoothing, healing 'camera' movement of the cleaner scene wins over its dimension of exposing us to the real gaze. Woody is restored to the point where his symbolic inscription, his name-of-the-father, disappears: the letters 'ANDY' on his sole are painted over, marking his exit from the symbolic order and complete entry into the imaginary one. One might say that he chooses the museum life out of compassion for the rest of his set (Jessie being traumatized by her life locked away in the stock), but the images of the film, showing his overwhelming enjoyment with his own image, tell another story: a subject being driven by the imaginary look, being caught in the limelight of the big Other.

If *Toy Story* can be said to tell the story of Woody symbolically 'castrating' Buzz, *Toy Story 2* could be said to tell the story of Buzz 'castrating' Woody. As I have already pointed out, though, they are castrated 'from' two different states: Buzz from the psychotic state of being the instrument of the big Other (the space control), Woody from the narcissist state of being the idol of big O (the public).

When Woody in *Toy Story* tells Buzz 'YOU ARE A TOY', it means 'you are not a space ranger'. When in *Toy Story 2* Buzz addresses exactly the same line to Woody, it means 'you are not a collector's item'. Whereas Buzz's castration throws him into femininity (as Sid's sister dresses him up as 'Mrs Nesbit'), Woody's castration throws him into mortality. Woody's choice between the glass coffin for exposition and the shaft through which his friends have come to save him, seems to be a choice between immortality and finitude.

In both the case of Woody and of Buzz, the 'castration' is symbolized by the loss of an arm. But they get their arms back on in different ways. In Buzz's case in a kind of magical operation performed by Sid's surrealistic constellations, gathering around him in a way that hides to the spectator what is happening, symbolizing perhaps that reparative phase of artistic creation à la Melanie Klein to which they seem in their very constitution to bear witness. In Woody's case the arm is sewn back on twice: the first time in the cleaner's perfect and invisible stitches, making it as good as (or even better than) new. The second time in Andy's clumsy sewing, stuffing the arm's filling unevenly, so the upper arm becomes much too thick. The point is that Woody finally likes Andy's clumsy reparation better than the cleaner's perfect one, and the 'mistake', the deformity of the upper arm, seems actually to be able to take on new values as a signifier: Woody poses as a bodybuilder, showing off his swelling 'biceps'. So, actually his signifier of 'castration', the deformed arm, becomes a sign of potency. Which may be what symbolic 'castration' is all about: gaining from your loss. Gaining access to language and symbolization, to that play of signifiers in which every phenomenon, even a deformed arm, is ready to be filled with new and never absolute meaning.

If *Toy Story* tells us the story of the psychotic subject becoming a split subject (a normal-neurotic toy . . .) through his fall, *Toy Story 2* tells us the story of the subject being tempted to congeal in imaginary perfection, but finally coming to terms with his imperfection, his fissure, being staged as the fissure between the imaginary look and the real gaze.

3

Sadism in the Kindergarten: *Toy Story 3*

Toy Story 3, to a large degree, takes up the themes of *Toy Story* and *Toy Story 2*: the question of vanity and mortality; the theme of the partial object, including the gaze; the problem of separation; the sadistic dimension of playing; the change between a neurotic and a psychotic constitution that once again the character of Buzz Lightyear has to undergo.

This chapter wants to claim that *Toy Story 3* depicts *the partial object as such* as that which animates the human subject, allegorized in the character of Mr Potato Head whose detachable partial objects seem in this film's rather original visual fantasies to be his very substance. The partial object as substance will be related to Lacan's conception of the independent partial object, 'the lamella', as a metaphor for libido. Supplementing Lacan's theory of the partial object with Melanie Klein's as well as with Winnicott's concept of 'the transitional object', the chapter further inquires into the film's depiction of children's play and creativity as partly sadistic. Finally, the chapter regards the day care in the film as an allegory of society as based on the organization of that monstrous surplus energy which may be still another answer to the question of the principle animating the human being.

In the beginning of *Toy Story 3* (Lee Unkrich, 2010) we meet the toy characters all packed in a box, as Andy, now a young man, is on his way to college and not playing with them anymore. The toys are deposited in the day care centre 'Sunnyside', only to find that the seemingly lovable leader of this seemingly idyllic place, the pink strawberry-scented (!) teddy bear Lotso (short for 'Lots-o'-Hugging', voiced by Ned Beatty), is a cruel tyrant, assigning the newcomers to the room of the youngest toddlers who play with them in an utterly ruthless way. Together with a horror-style, dead-eyed, old-fashioned doll, 'Big Baby', and a bunch of other weak or villainous toys, including a hilariously smug and stupid Ken doll (Michael Keaton), the pink bear rules the place by methods of torture and imprisons our friends in plastic baskets as they try to revolt. Through flashbacks we learn how Lotso and Big Baby are traumatized by their former owner's forgetting and rejecting them. The villains violently switch Buzz Lightyear (Tim Allen) into his demo mode, turning him back to his psychotic space ranger state, making him the prison guard of his friends, and he even has to pass through a state of being a silly and Spanish-speaking romantic flamenco hero, before regaining his normal self. Trying to escape, our heroes find themselves, together with the cruel pink teddy bear, on their way to final extermination in the incinerators of the dumping ground. The friends holding hands on their way to the lethal flames is a truly sinister scene reminiscent of catastrophe or even Holocaust films. But of course the toys are finally saved and end up with Andy, who entrusts them to the care of a small, charming girl talented with the same gift of playing as his younger self. In the epilogue we see how Barbie (Jodi Benson) and Ken, the new leaders of the toy society in 'Sunnyside', have turned it into a fair and modern working society, in which toys take turns doing the hard work, and are recompensed by beach holidays in the sandbox and disco parties in Barbie and Ken's dream house . . .

Vanity and mortality

In his book *Seeing Things*, Alan Ackerman states the common theme of *Toy Story* and *Toy Story 2* to be 'the mortality of toys' (Ackerman 2011: 98). This theme obviously continues in *Toy Story 3*: the whole plot revolves around the passing of time and the toys facing the threat of going to the dump. As Ackerman observes, the *Toy Story* characters are obsessed with the idea of mortality, but also they are constantly resurrected, coming to life again and again. The obsession with mortality and resurrection is to Ackerman partly a distinctive human trait, partly a metaphysical aspiration ('something infinite emerges from the man-made' (98)), but primarily he sees it as having to do with the characters' being commercial products, commodities, supposed to be reproduced again and again in all kinds of materials and media ('To be a toy in a Disney movie is to be reproduced' (115)), in a ghostlike manner. The very fact of making the *Toy Story* characters come to life again in a third movie could be seen as part of this logic of resurrection/reproduction.

Ackerman refers the resurrectability/reproducibility of the toys to Marx's definition of the commodity as 'a very strange thing, abounding in metaphysical subtleties and theological niceties' (Marx 1990: 163), and he writes:

> Apparently made of dead matter (plastic and chemicals) these toys enact a fantasy of continual resurrection, an idealizing revival of the dead, not only in the game of the individual child but also in the processes of production and marketing, of which both movies are highly self-conscious.
>
> (Ackerman 2011: 100–1)

The films' reflection of their own mechanisms of distribution and marketing is also an issue in *Toy Story 3*. For instance when Buzz goes into his 'Spanish mode' and we hear him speak in fluent Castilian Spanish, this reflects the fact that the *Toy Story* films and characters have been distributed worldwide and translated into other languages. Actually, in a kind of loop between production, marketing and reproduction, the Spanish actor whom Pixar chose to voice Buzz had already voiced him in Spanish TV commercials for the *Toy Story* merchandise.

Ackerman's criticism of a capitalist logic of reproducible commodities at work in the theme of recurring resurrection and reanimation is sharp and interesting. Yet the plot of *Toy Story 3* also implies a criticism of this commercial logic of reproduction. Toys do seem to be reproducible and replaceable, when the girl Daisy, in the film's melodramatic flashback, has lost her beloved teddy bear, Lotso, and her parents just buy her a new one. Yet this replacement is depicted as something cruel, erasing the singularity of Lotso, and the whole plot seems to carry a message of keeping and recycling instead of throwing away and replacing: the final heroine is the little girl Bonnie who takes over Andy's old toys and gives to them a new life. There may even be said to be an ironic clash between the figures' uniqueness as characters of the film, and their infinite reproducibility as merchandise, and between the film's message of keeping and recycling, and the logic of cheap, reproducible plastic toys in which it partakes through marketing and merchandise.

The lamella

The theme of the partial object, already present in *Toy Story* and *Toy Story 2*, is taken further in *Toy Story 3* through the characters of Mr and Mrs Potato Head (Don Rickles and Estelle Harris). In a quite imaginative invention Mr Potato Head is transformed into Mr Tortilla Head, as he detaches all of his partial objects (nose, ears, mouth, eyes, feet, etc.) from his potato-body, reattaching them to a flat tortilla, allowing him to slip under doors. This results in a really fascinating visual fantasy: a very fragile body, insecurely moving, difficult to uphold, and finally fragmenting as a pigeon picks in it with its beak. (The pigeon is called 'Feathers' in Mr Tortilla Head's address: 'What are you looking at, Feathers?' Even this address, by the trope of metonymy, names the whole object, the pigeon, after its partial and detachable objects, the feathers.)

The tortilla gag seems partly to belong to the meta-commentaries on their own technique that the Pixar films like to make. *Toy Story 3* is Pixar's first film in 3D, and the relation between potato and tortilla seems to mirror the relationship between 3D and 2D. In his book on the voice in cinema, Michel Chion remarks that the concept of 'silent movie' was retroactively invented, at the time when talking movies had become the norm (Chion 1999: 7). One might imagine a future in which we analogously will call 2D movies 'flat films', as 3D has become the norm. Mr Tortilla Head is Mr Potato Head as flat film.

In the commentary track, director Lee Unkrich tells how the figure of Mr Potato Head triggered a fantasy about his parts constantly detaching themselves from one body and being in search for another. This fantasy led to the figure of Mr Tortilla Head, who passes through yet another body, a phallic or faecal squash, before returning to his plastic potato shell. Unkrich tells how the crew had other ideas of possible bodies for Mr Potato Head: rotten fruits, an apple with a worm, in a kind of very infantile fantasizing about the body and what it could be.

The interesting thing about this idea is that it turns the partial objects into that which constitutes the subjects. The partial objects are not just attributes to Mr Potato Head's bodily substance, rather they seem to be the substance themselves, ready to occupy any convenient body.

In seminar XI, Lacan (1979: 197) introduces something he calls 'the lamella' as a version of the Freudian partial object. In biology a 'lamella' is a disc-like cellular structure, in mycology a papery rib under the cap of the mushroom. Lacan's lamella is an autonomous, immortal, indivisible part capable of moving everywhere. It is a kind of leftover from the production of the subject: 'what the sexed being loses in sexuality', or with a biological image, that which escapes when the membranes of the egg are broken by the sperm. The image of the broken egg develops into a joke: 'one can do it with an egg as easily as with a man, namely the *hommelette*, or the lamella'. Lacan here makes his famous pun on *homme* (man) and *hommelette* (little man or omelette). From the egg comes the little man, that is the infant as an omelette, a kind of undivided, undefined mass. But with the little man a kind of leftover is born (Lacan evokes the placenta as an image for this (198)). This leftover, the lamella, is 'easier to animate' than the little man 'in whose head one always had to place a homunculus to get it working' (197).

So the lamella is animated all by itself: it does not need an 'animus' or animating principle, it *is* the animating principle all in itself. It is kind of scary, Lacan assures us, by evoking a horror-movie-like image: 'Suppose it comes and envelopes your face while you are quietly asleep . . .' (197). Lacan defines the lamella as the libido, and libido as 'pure life instinct': 'immortal life, or irrepressible life, life that has need of no organ, simplified, indestructible life' (198).

Žižek remarks that that which Lacan here calls 'life instinct' is actually what Freud calls 'death drive': 'We should bear in mind that "death drive" is, paradoxically, the Freudian name for its very opposite, for the way immortality appears within psychoanalysis: for an uncanny excess of life, an "undead" urge that persists beyond the (biological) circle of life and death, generation and corruption' (Žižek 2006: 63). This 'undead urge' persisting beyond death, 'the hand from the grave', is a classical horror device, which is quoted in *Toy Story 3* as the teddy bear Lotso stretches out his arm from the garbage container, in which we just thought that he was buried, and drags our heroes down.

The lamella is that in man which escapes his submission to the cycle of reproduction. Hereby Lacan and Žižek stress an important psychoanalytic point: the Freudian 'libido' or sexual drive is not a biological drive of reproduction, it rather conceptualizes the fact that we have sex far beyond reproduction, that sexual drive seems to have no goal or motor but itself, just like the 'lamella'.

The 'lamella', the autonomous partial object having an indestructible life of its own, is thus Lacan's metaphor for that 'uncanny excess of life' persisting beyond individual death that Freud calls 'the death drive'.

Visually, the tortilla might seem an adequate image of the Lacanian 'lamella', being a flat and disc-like structure, not unlike the Host served at the holy communion, interpreted by Slavoj Žižek as exactly some kind of 'lamella' from the body of Christ: the immortal, indestructible part (Žižek 2009: 289). Structurally, though, it is rather Mr Potato Head's partial objects that are 'lamellas', partial objects having a life of their own beyond the bodies to which they are only temporarily attached.

In *How to Read Lacan*, Žižek defines the lamella as a version of the Freudian partial object and further as 'a weird organ that is magically autonomized, surviving without the body whose organ it should have been' (2006: 62). Žižek's examples are the hand that wanders around alone in surrealist films and the cat's grin that remains after the cat has vanished in *Alice in Wonderland*, but the description seems to fit Mr Potato Head's partial objects as well.

Mrs Potato Head, on her side, is in this film a perfect image of the gaze as a partial object. Her eye is literally depicted as a detachable partial object as it is left behind in Andy's room while the toys are in Sunnyside Day Care. From her distance she can actually establish a contact with her left-behind eye, but this implies a dizzy tunnel movement, graphically illustrated by whirling coloured spirals reminiscent of the whirls in Hitchcock's *Vertigo*, showing us the vertigo that would result if one could really take in one's own gaze as an object.

Mrs Potato Head's relationship with her detached eye even resembles the Christian God's relationship with his son as it is described by Žižek when he writes that God has pulled out his eye and thrown it into the world as Jesus Christ, so that it can look at him, or so that God can look at himself through it (Žižek 2009: 80).

Thus Mr Potato/Tortilla Head gives us yet another image of that which animates the human being, not only the partial objects of gaze and voice, but partial objects of all kinds regarded as Lacanian 'lamellas'. The lamella being an instance of that 'life instinct' that is the Freudian death drive, Mr Tortilla Head is actually an image of the death drive, or 'the uncanny excess of life' as the animating principle.

Potatoes

In Sianne Ngai's brilliant chapter (from *Ugly Feelings*) on 'animatedness' as a marker of racial or ethnic otherness, we meet another interesting animated potato. Ngai's main example of the connection between animation and racialization is the 3D 'foamation' TV series *The PJs*, and central to her argument is a scene in which two of the characters (poorly) animate a potato to be baby-Jesus. *The PJs* features African-American residents of an urban subsidized housing project, and its dolls with outsized plastic heads and grotesquely big facial traits have been accused of representing racially offensive stereotypes. Ngai finds the show's representation of race to be less simple, though, and even to have a critical dimension. She finds this critical dimension not the least in the show's very excess of animation and its foregrounding its own artificiality, thereby also exposing the artificiality of racial stereotypes (Ngai 2005: 104). The self-reflexive and excessive dimension of the animation in *The PJs* are to Ngai clearly expressed in 'the slippery mouth syndrome': the phenomenon of the figures' detachable mouth (each character has a set of 40 replacement mouths) moving to the side of the face in asynchrony with the speech, producing 'an unintended, excess animatedness' in which the racially-symbolically overdetermined big mouth threatens to fly off the body (116). The 'slippery mouth syndrome' culminates when all facial features slide off the potato baby-Jesus, which Ngai reads as a figure of the show's self-reflection on its own (crude) animation technique. Ngai celebrates the potato scene as the show's 'mise en abyme of its own mode of production, in which the crudeness and distortion attributed to its foamation characters became hyperbolized in a very poorly animated potato' (122).

It is one of Ngai's points that animation seems to chop up the body into its parts. She shows this mechanism to be at work already in abolitionist literature. As explained in this book's introduction she links this chopping up of the body to marking racial otherness, for instance in *Uncle Tom's Cabin* (1852) when Tom's lips seem to take on a life of their own as he is animated by 'the language of Scripture' (Ngai 2005: 97).

The potato characters in *Toy Story 3* might be seen as a reminiscence of this connection between animation and chopping up the body. Here all facial features as well as other partial objects not only threaten to fly off, but do fly off all the time. The racializing side of animation does not seem to be present in the characters of Mr and Mrs Potato Head who do not appear as ethnically specified. They do appear as gendered, though, and in the case of Mrs Potato Head one might observe a kind of excessive, aggressive femininity going hand-in-hand with her excessive animatedness.

The question is whether the self-reflection on animation inherent in the figure of Mr Potato/Tortilla Head has some of the critical potential that Ngai finds in the potato from *The PJs*?

Whereas the poorly animated PJ potato could be seen as mocking and exposing the (racializing-animating) technique of the whole series, the Pixar potato in its meta-technical dimension rather belongs to the recurring Pixar theme of mocking more primitive techniques, thereby celebrating the superiority of computer animation. In its first 3D movie, Pixar mocks 2D through the flatness of a tortilla as opposed to the volume of a potato. Animating a potato by sticking detachable partial objects into it could further be seen as a kind of basic, primitive animation, completely surpassed by the perfect computer animation of Mr and Mrs Potato Head whose parts always smoothly and if by themselves end up fitting into their right places. Still, on the allegorical level, the swaying, stumbling Tortilla Man, animated by detachable partial objects, gives us a counterpoint to the smoothness of the computer technique: an image of a fragile subjectivity animated by the death drive. The fantasy of the detachable partial objects as the very substance of the subject is a counterpoint to the smooth body image provided by the Pixar technique.

Separation and playing

The most obvious lesson taught in *Toy Story 3* is how to deal with separation by carrying mentally with you the person that you are separated from. In the main story the toys, specifically Woody, have to learn to separate from Andy, and in the side story the same goes for Andy's mother. Near the end of the film, there is a scene in which Andy's mother enters his empty room just before his departure, expressing a sadness that cannot leave any mother's eyes dry. 'I wish I could always be with you', she tells her son. 'You will be, Mom', he answers. Woody watches and hears this scene, and from the expression of his face we are clearly to understand that he has an important insight. If somebody should have missed this, they will be taught when putting on the commentary track in which director Lee Unkrich does not refrain from using the word 'catharsis' to describe Woody's insight in this scene: 'There is a way to be with Andy without physically being with him.'

To psychoanalysis dealing with separation is actually the central existential challenge, from the first separation from the maternal body, to the last separation from life itself. In Lacan's view the anxiety of castration (that is, separation) is overruled by the anxiety of being too close to the maternal body, from which separation liberates us. The tool of liberation is language; the liberation of saying 'mother' instead of being in close and wordless contact with mother.

To object relation theory, the way to learn how to handle separation leads through the 'potential space' and the 'transitional object'. 'Potential space' is Winnicott's concept for the space of playing (and fiction and arts); the space in which we invent and imagine while on some level being conscious that this is not reality (without this consciousness we enter into the zone of psychosis). The 'transitional objects' are the props of potential space, pre-eminently the objects, be they toys or other things, in which children invest their fantasies and feelings while gradually and relatively becoming independent from their primary caregiving person. Winnicott stresses, though, that his 'transitional object' is less an object than 'a paradox': 'What I am referring to [...] is not the cloth or the teddy bear that the baby uses – not so much the object used as the use of an object' (Winnicott 1971: xi).

The force of Winnicott's idea is the autonomy that he gives to potential space, making of it a primary space of human consciousness that cannot be reduced to a substitutive or sublimating activity. The transitional object has a value of its own; it is not that the child clings to the teddy bear when the mother is absent and throws it away when she is present. The teddy bear stays important even with the mother present. This autonomy of the potential space and the transitory object makes of Winnicott an heir to Friedrich Schiller and his idea of the *Spieltrieb* as a third *Trieb* (drive) in the human being besides nature and moral.

The *Toy Story* movies basically celebrate the activity of playing. The opening scene of *Toy Story 3* once again shows us the art of animation as a continuation of the child's play. It is a perfectly animated train-chase Western scene turning into some kind of space fiction, starring Woody, Buzz, Jessie, the Potato Heads and 'Evil Dr Pork Chop'. We learn, though, that this perfectly animated scene is actually Andy's handheld play. The complete illusion of being in the scenario of an action film is to be understood as Andy's illusion, created by his playful imagination. Thus the child's play is shown as the source of the animators' art. Furthermore, Andy's play is framed by the gaze of the adult; the image is constructed as if seen through his filming mother's video camera. From being completely immersed in the illusion of the play, we are put at a double distance: the toys are handheld by Andy who is filmed by his mother's handheld camera. The idealized image of the child completely engulfed in his play may also be an illusion of the envious adult who suffers from the feeling of being at a distance. The child is staged as 'the subject supposed to believe', this kind of big Other needed to sustain the nostalgic gaze, as we saw in the analysis of *Toy Story 2*. Nostalgia is a fundamental theme in *Toy Story 3*, not least the parents' nostalgia for their children's childhood.

Sadism and creation

In a striking parallel to *Toy Story*, *Toy Story 3* opposes the caring and considerate way of handling toys to the sadist-aggressive one. The opposition in *Toy Story* between the loving Andy and the sadist Sid is in *Toy Story 3* completely repeated as the opposition between the Barbarian toddlers in 'The Caterpillar Room' and the elder considerate children in 'The Butterfly Room'. The Caterpillar toddlers soil and fragment the toys in a completely uninhibited oral-anal-sadistic way: Jessie is dipped into paint and used as a pencil, Mr Potato Head's body parts end up in a really disgusting snotty kid's mouth and nostrils, Dinosaur's tail is broken off, the small green Martians are squeezed under another kid's buttocks, Hamm has his cork pulled out and his stomach filled with various small objects, Buzz finds himself facing the giant wet tongue of a kid who is eager to lick him. In the Butterfly room, on the contrary, we see the elder children nursing, hugging and playing constructively with the toys. On the commentary track Unkrich morally-pedagogically explains the opposition as one between 'abuse' and 'imaginative play', seemingly ignorant of the wisdom expressed on the commentary track to *Toy Story*: the animators' identification with Sid's experimental, sadistic way of playing rather than Andy's carefulness.

The oral attack on Buzz is shot in a rather spectacular way, changing between objective and subjective shot: the point of view of the kid and the point of view of Buzz, being mediated by Buzz's transparent visor functioning as a mirror. The kid's mouth approaches Buzz, and we end up in a full-screen close-up of the fleshy tongue surrounded by a halo of drool, teeth and lips, based (as we can learn from the commentary track) on the animators' meticulous studies of real drool. This is a complete surrealist image, a kind of portrait of the subject (Buzz) as a dim figure projected on the screen of the tongue, framed by drool, teeth and lips. The first things appearing in the mirror of the tongue are Buzz's eyes, so for a moment we have a kind of confusion of sight and orality, eyes framed by lips. It might even look like a birth scene, Buzz's face appearing in the vaginal form of the open mouth. The subject born from the prospect of being orally engulfed. This is a moment of exploiting the possibilities of the computer technique to give us impossible shots, transcending mimetic realism, taking us closer to the real. It gives us the object's view and totally engulfs us in the toddler's oral universe, just as the animators have literally immersed themselves in oral liquidity by studying drool.

The Caterpillar room takes us back to the original universe of cartoons and silent movies, the pre-Oedipal universe before verbal language, guilt, sexuality and death have made their entrance into the life of the subject. The universe of slapstick where the characters, however violently treated, will always survive and recover.

To object relation theory the toddler's sadist–aggressive handling of his transitional objects is not 'abuse', but a vital and indispensable state in the

Figure 3 Buzz Lightyear in the mirror of the tongue. From *Toy Story 3* (Lee Unkrich, 2010) © Pixar.

formation of the subject. In his essay 'Use of an Object and Relating', Winnicott states the subject's aggressive attack on the object as a necessary precondition for the establishment of the object as something external to the subject, something that cannot be reduced to the subject's projection. The object only gains its external quality, and can then be the object of love, when having survived the subject's aggressive attacks. To Winnicott this destruction is not a one-time event, but something that has to be regularly repeated:

> From now on the subject says: 'Hullo, object!' 'I destroyed you.' 'I love you.' 'You have value for me because of your survival of my destruction of you.' 'While I am loving you I am all the time destroying you in (unconscious) fantasy.'
>
> (Winnicott 1971: 120–1)

So, Winnicott's thesis is rather radical: without the destructive drive in the subject there would be no external reality (125). To Winnicott, aggression is not the reaction to a frustrating reality; on the contrary, aggression creates reality (as that which survives aggression's attacks). The logic is not: when we cannot have it our way, because we bump into the wall of reality, we become furious; but rather: because we are furious, we bump into the wall of reality, as that which survives our furious attack. As Barbara Johnson shows, Winnicott here actually rhetorically animates the transitional object by apostrophizing it: 'Hullo object!' The apostrophe is in poetry the animating figure number one; it is the figure of talking to a thing as if it were a human. Winnicott not only defines the transitional object as something in between the inanimate and the animate, he also rhetorically performs its animation (Johnson 2008: 103).

Whereas Sid in *Toy Story* (actually making a reappearance in *Toy Story 3*, as garbage man!) is partly a portrait of the artist and as the result of his sadism is presented as surrealist sculptures, the toddlers' sadism with the toys seems in *Toy Story 3* to be depicted as pure destruction. The film's mode is first and foremost nostalgic.

Sunnyside Day Care is a universe in which even God seems to be a sadist. The place has an 'eye in the sky' of its own: the monkey guarding the surveillance screens, emitting a terrible, mechanical cry and clashing its cymbals whenever an irregularity is observed. The monkey is staged in a way reminiscent of the mummy in Hitchcock's *Psycho* as we approach it (with Woody) from the back and have a shock as it turns around. As it is completely wrapped up in white Scotch tape it literally resembles a mummy. As Hitchcock's mummy it seems to be a configuration of what psychoanalysis calls the sadistic superego: the controlling, regulating instance not as rational morality, but as a primitive kind of mechanics screaming at any autonomous initiative that the subject might take. The first psychoanalyst to point to this sadistic component of the superego was Melanie Klein. To Klein, the foundation of the superego is the infant's fear that the object (mother) might take revenge on the aggressive attacks that the subject fantasizes of causing to it (Klein 1998a).

The most horrible figure in *Toy Story 3* remains the infant. Big Baby's lack of verbal language and grotesque mixture of baby body and brute adult behaviour, mechanics and organic life make him really creepy. In a less horrible, but still monstrous mode, the preverbal toddlers in the Caterpillar room give us the image of human children as a monstrous surplus of energy that will make the theme of *Monsters, Inc.* The problem of handling this monstrous surplus energy could be said to be the political problem of Sunnyside regarded as a community. In the epilogue the solution to this problem is a distribution of work which looks quite much like Western society today: the toys take turns to be objects of the toddlers' brute handling, Barbie encourages them swinging her cheerleader pom-poms, and the toys get to spend their spare time on the beach in the sandbox or at disco parties in Ken and Barbie's dream house. The class division is clear: the brute and clumsy toys are the workers, while Ken and Barbie are the managers.

The horror and sadism of *Toy Story 3* reside in its theme of the partial object, which partly appears as a Lacanian lamella (a very creepy thing!), partly as a transitional object supposed to arouse and survive the subject's sadist aggression. The evil figures of the movie could be seen as configurations of the obscene superego as well as of the most monstrous monster in the Pixar universe: the human child, to whom we shall return in the analysis of *Monsters, Inc.* (Chapter 5).

4

Entertainment as Warfare: *A Bug's Life*

In *A Bug's Life* the animating principle seems to be that wish for recognition that is a dominant theme in Lacan, taken from Hegel. Another principle animating the characters of the film seems to be the pun. This chapter relates this to Lacan's view of the pun as the play of the signifiers animating the human subject. *A Bug's Life* puts the signifier into play not only in the verbal puns (cf. the pun on 'bug' in the title), but also in the visual allegory that travels through the film: the rock as an object of exchange and sign of recognition which has its meaning not from its substance, use value or reference, but from its very circulation.

A Bug's Life (John Lasseter, Andrew Stanton, 1998) is a story of emancipation from oppression. A tribe of ants, living on an island, work hard to pick seed not only for themselves, but also for the grasshoppers who come to collect their part each year when the first leaf falls. The hero of the film, Flik (Dave Foley), is a creative and innovative ant who develops a mechanical machine to ease the harvesting work. His first machine provokes disaster, though, as it hits and spreads the collected seeds just as the grasshoppers are arriving to pick them up. Their brute leader, Hopper (Kevin Spacey), gives the ants the rest of the season to re-collect their tax of seeds, but Flik goes to the city and returns with a troupe of circus bugs, mistaking them for warriors who are then to help the ants fight the grasshoppers. Surpassing a number of hindrances and detours, the ants finally chase away the grasshoppers and can go on collecting seeds only for themselves, their work efficiency being improved by Flik's invention. This tale of emancipation is intertwined with a love story, as Flik and the ant princess Atta (Julia Louis-Dreyfus) gradually become a couple, both of them learning to be self-confident and less afraid to make mistakes (as mistakes even prove to turn out productive). The change from the rule of the grasshoppers to the autonomy of the ants seems to reflect a change from a feudal master/slave system to a more democratic system in which the creative individual's technological innovations play an important part. Interestingly, not only technological innovation and individual courage, but also entertainment (the circus troupe) is crucial to the process of emancipation, which may be seen as a celebration of Pixar's own qualities.

Pun

The film and its characters seem to a certain degree to be animated by the pun. That is, the pun seems to be at work in the animators' invention of theme, plot and characters, and also seems to be an important animating principle in the characters as they are portrayed. The title itself is a pun on the word 'bug' which does not only mean an insect, but also an error in a computer program causing it to produce unintended and unexpected results. The film's plot shows us that such errors can be productive: the ants' emancipation from the grasshoppers starts with Flik scattering the seeds by mistake and is carried on through his mistaking the circus troupe for an army of warriors. This celebration of the creative error points to the technique of computer animation itself, in which errors may actually prove productive. Such as, for instance, in the simulated computer game in *Toy Story 2* in which little rocks are flying around Buzz. From the commentary track you learn that they were not supposed to, they should just be on the ground, but the animators liked and kept the effect that was actually a technical mistake.

Even the quite dominant queer theme of the film, the character of the male ladybird (called by the androgynous name of Francis, voiced by Denis Leary) mistaken for a woman, seems to grow out of a pun: 'ladybird' connoting femininity and resembling the word 'ladyboy'.

The pun is central to psychoanalysis. At a press conference in Rome in 1974 Lacan even claimed the pun to be the key to psychoanalysis: 'I do attribute an enormous importance to puns, you know. This seems to me to be the key to psychoanalysis.'

Lacan's own concepts are often actually puns. *Hommelette* meaning both 'little man' and 'omelette' as a concept for the infant in its state of undifferentiation, before the symbolic order cuts the line between child and (m)other. *Lituraterre* playing with the letters in order to make us understand that literature takes care of the letters that are litter as well as dust (*terre*) to pragmatic, communicative language (that is, pragmatic language throws away the materiality of language, ignoring that the stuff that words are made of actually has an important significance, which is the very principle of the pun). Babbling *à la cantonade*, which means the small child babbling, but already in a way that captures the intonations and distinctions of language, thus anticipating what Lacan (à *la can*tonade) would claim about language as the differentiating principle. *Sînthome* punning on *Saint homme* (holy man) and *Saint Thomas* (the holy Thomas), meaning what happens when you incarnate, identify with your 'symptom' which then becomes something saint (like Jesus's wound incarnated the existential wound in every human being).

But how and why could puns be the key to psychoanalysis? Well, Lacan's own pun 'Lalangue' might give us a key to this. 'Lalangue' which is the contraction of 'La langue', the language or the tongue, but stresses the lallation, the babbling redundancy, as the very principle of language, the giving away to the letters and sounds (the litter and dust) of language which are carrying the things that you say without intending to say them, that is, the unconscious.

The babbling language stuttering the same syllables, which may be seen as an instance of 'lalangue', actually has an important plot function in the film. When the queen says 'Help us, don't help us', the words are repeated and at the same time transformed by Flik: 'help us to help'. When she states that 'we never leave the island, there are bigger bugs out there' the same thing happens; Flik repeats her words 'never leave', 'exactly, bigger bugs', turning the queen's prohibition into the idea that makes the plot move: if I leave the island I can find bigger bugs to help us. What seems pure redundancy, the meaningless repetition of syllables, actually develops into a new meaning, a new idea.

'Lalangue' seems at work also when Flik corrects his own language in order to mask the circus bugs as warriors: 'The warriors have called for a secret meeting to plan for the circus – uh, circumventing the oncoming hordes so they can trapeze – trap them with ease.' 'Circus/circumventing', 'trapeze/trap them with ease' – words producing words by pure resemblance of letters and sounds, but at the same time producing meaning, making us start wondering whether there might be an actual resemblance between entertainment and warfare.

The pun is the key to psychoanalysis because it makes it clear that our language carries unintended, unconscious meanings. Or to put it more strongly: language is the medium of the unconscious. Unconscious connections and structures cling to the seemingly meaningless 'material' of language, language as letters and sounds. Lacan insists on this materiality of the *signifiant* ('signifier'), a term that he takes from the founding father of structuralist linguistics, Ferdinand de Saussure, who divides the verbal sign into 'signifier' (the letters and sounds that compose the word, for instance the word 'tree') and 'signified' (the concept or mental image that we get from the word, for instance the image of a tree). Now, the materiality of the signifier is in pragmatic, communicative language thought to be unimportant, meaningless; what matters is the signified, no matter of which letters and sounds it is composed. This is exactly why messages from the unconscious can hide in the material traces and patterns of the signifier. Perhaps this is the most important lesson to be taken from Freud's 'Interpretation of Dreams'. When Freud interprets dreams, what he does is actually very much to follow the trace of the material signifier, to associate from one word to another that consist of partly the same material, the same letters. To understand this, one must first be aware that the dreams that Freud (and psychoanalysis as a clinical practice) interprets are actually texts: they are verbalized dreams (reported on the couch).

To give one example: when Freud interprets his dream on the botanical monography, in which he dreams that he has written such a monography and turns its pages, the stepping stones of his interpretations are a series of words and names including the syllable 'ko' or 'kö'. His first association is the monography on '**co**caine' that he wrote when he was young, propagating the anaesthetic function of the drug. This makes him think of Dr **Ko**ller who introduced cocaine as an anaesthetic and did not refer to Freud, thus taking the honour of the discovery. From Dr **Ko**ller his association moves on to a fantasy about being in**co**gnito operated on for glau**co**ma, which makes him remember that his father actually was anaesthetized by Dr **Ko**ller when operated on for glau**co**ma by Dr **Kö**nigstein with whom Freud had had a conversation the evening before the dream. Thus the little syllable 'ko' leads through words and names that tell the story of Freud's relationships with other men, notably fatherly figures, a story of rivalry and (lack of/wish for) recognition (Freud 1953: 170–2).

Another example may be the Wolfman's chain of associations as reported by Freud in his case study. The Wolfman has a phobia for butterflies. In Russian, his mother tongue, butterfly is called 'Babusjka' which reminds him of the name of the maid who aroused his sexual fantasies as a child, 'Grusja', meaning also 'pear' which through the association of yellow rims makes him think of wasps, in German 'Wespe' which, if you remove a wing ('W'), sounds like 'S. P.', the initials of his own name: Sergei Pankejeff. Some of the associations are produced by semantic reference (such as the likeness between pear and wasp), but others have the quality that highlights the material signifier as the carrier of unconscious connections: Babusjka/Grusja, Wespe/SP (Freud 1955b: 90–4).

Metaphor concretized

The title 'A Bug's Life' is not only a pun, but actually seems to describe the operation of its own punning: it gives life to the dead metaphor of 'bug', animates it, makes of it a walking, living character, the ant Flik. The same operation is at work when the walking stick from the circus troupe is used to incarnate a verbal expression: one of his fellow artists slaps him and announces: 'slap stick!' Again, this joke seems to be naming its own performance, being itself an instance of slapstick.

Even in the opening scene the dramatic action seems to be determined by the concretization of metaphor. 'I am always acting like the sky is falling', Princess Atta says – and then it actually does, as a straw (giant compared to the ants) falls. Even the 'gap in the line' provoked by the falling leaf earlier does have a quality of concretized metaphor; as a more abstract expression a 'gap in the line' (some irregularity, something missing, a hole in the line of signifiers) is often what initiates the plot, but here the gap is a concrete gap in the concrete line of ants.

The concretization of metaphor, more in the mode of misunderstanding than pun, is important to the development of the plot, as the circus artists declare: 'When your grasshopper friends get here, we are gonna knock them dead!', reinforcing the confusion between warriors and circus artists.

Exchanging rocks

The double meaning residing in common metaphors seems here to carry a hidden social analytical point: entertainment as weapon. When the circus bugs declare that 'our troupe guarantees a performance like no other' and 'we are gonna knock them dead!' the military metaphors invading their discourse testify to this point. Our language carries the structures and connections that we are not consciously aware of, individually as well as culturally. The plot of the film confirms that entertainment may be used as a part of strategic warfare. In order to give the ants the possibility to prepare their secret weapon, the artificial bird, the circus artists distract and pacify the grasshoppers by performing a show. If comedy is here a weapon, it is comedy as distraction and pacification.

What is concretized in *A Bug's Life* seems generally to be the abstraction of language itself. This happens not least in the exchange of a rock as a reoccurring and a little mysterious motif. In the beginning of the film, Flik shows a rock to the small ant princess Dot, telling her to pretend it is a seed, in order to illustrate how his machine functions. Later, as Flik in a moment of crisis is sitting depressed in the circus wagon, Dot brings him another rock, telling him the same thing: 'Pretend it's a seed, okay?' This gesture mystifies the circus bugs around them: 'Hey, what's with the rock?' the ladybird asks – 'Must be an ant thing', the stick replies. At the end of the film the praying mantis magician Manny (Jonathan Harris) imitates the gesture by giving to the Princess a rock wrapped in a leaf. Now the ants are mystified: 'What's with the rock?' one ant asks – 'Must be a circus thing', his neighbour answers.

The seemingly pointless gesture of exchanging rocks, which gains significance from imitation and repetition, seems to illustrate the basic principle of language as understood by Lacan. In the text *Fonction et champ de la parole et du language en psychanalyse* ('The Function and Field of Speech and Language in Psychoanalysis') Lacan suggests that language begins with gifts that are meant to be useless: 'vases made to remain empty, shields too heavy to be carried, sheaves that will dry out, lances that are thrust into the ground'. Thus the 'neutralization by means of the signifier' might be 'the nature of language', and we may see the beginning of language 'among sea swallows [...] in the fish they pass each other from beak to beak' (Lacan 2006: 225). Whereas the rock in the beginning becomes a signifier because it is made to stand for another thing ('Pretend it's a seed'), it later illustrates the social origin of the signifier as a 'neutralized', useless circulating object of exchange.

Figure 4 What's with the rock? From *A Bug's Life* (John Lasseter) © Walt Disney Pictures/Pixar Animation Studios.

The structuralist anthropologist Claude Levy-Strauss claimed that human communities are based on the exchange of presents – objects, women, money. Lacan insists that also words constitute such socially formative objects of exchange. This is one of the reasons why he makes his infamous claim: 'The Unconscious is structured like a language.' The rules regulating our exchange of words mirror to Lacan the rules regulating our families and communities, and he claims that Levy-Strauss, when suggesting the implication of those rules of value and exchange, is 'conquering the very terrain in which Freud situates the unconscious' (Lacan 2006: 236). This testifies to Lacan's conception of the unconscious as something of a sociolinguistic nature: the grammar regulating our basic social structures is also the grammar regulating our language, and this grammar is our unconscious, a way of structuring, ordering, valuating our position and relations.

The equivalence and interchangeability between seed and rock may be seen as also derived from the technology of computer animation in which isomorphic forms (as well as surfaces of equal quality) are reused as different objects.

Multiplication

The line 'Pretend it's a seed' has a second echo in the film, in the scene where we are at the grasshoppers' place, a messy Mexican bar, politically incorrectly associating the grasshoppers with Mexicans as well as Hell's Angels. In order to illustrate how one rebellious, powerless ant may multiply into a powerful crowd of ants he takes a grain from a bottle lying upside down, declaring: 'Let's pretend this grain is one puny little ant.' Throwing it at his men, demonstrating that one puny little grain/ant does not hurt, he then pulls the cork and releases from the bottle a whole avalanche of grains, burying a few of the frightened grasshoppers. The point is clear: 'These puny little ants outnumber us a hundred to one, and if they ever find out, there goes our way of life.' This is exactly what happens in the end when all ants stand up as a powerful mass and finally defeat the grasshoppers.

The principle of multiplication is not only a political theme of the film, but also a technical principle of computer animation. Notably in the scenes from the underground cave of the ants we clearly have this feeling of multiplication: the principal ants acting in the foreground, being multiplied by the numerous ants forming the depth of the background. (In one case the multiplication is staged as a question of multi-perspective, that is when we have shots from the point of view of the fly.)

Thus one might wonder whether the rebellious multitude in *A Bug's Life* is the result of democratic revolutionary thought, or rather of the technique of reproducibility. The rebellious force in the film is on the one side the creative individualist (Flik), while on the other side it is the crowd formed by a homogenizing technique of reproduction. So does the film not rather confirm the creative capitalism that has produced it than contain any subversive potential? With a term taken from Judith Halberstam, the question could be put in this way: does *A Bug's Life* have Pixarvolt?

Pixarvolt

'Pixarvolt' is Judith Halberstam's term for that revolutionary energy which she extracts from animated films (not only from Pixar) that use 'Pixar technologies' (which she opposes to the linear temporality of the traditional animation technique) and deal with 'themes of revolution and transformation'. Those films, according to Halberstam, depict queer, cross-generational and cross-species alliances between odd creatures, be it animals (*Over the Hedge*), fish (*Finding Nemo*) or sponges (*SpongeBob SquarePants*), getting together in communities opposed to capitalist exploitation and alternative to the nuclear family. Pixarvolt is, according to Halberstam, 'unsettling and perverse animal narratives', 'stories of collective action, anti-capitalist critique, group bonding', presenting us with 'alternative imaginings of community, space, embodiment and responsibility', 'connect[ing] individualism to selfishness [and] untrammeled consumption', 'opposing it with a collective mentality'. Just like non-Pixar films may contain 'Pixarvolt', not all of Pixar's films have it: 'Two thematics can transform a potential Pixarvolt film into a tame and conventional cartoon: family and romance' – which excludes films such as *Ratatouille* and *The Incredibles* from Halberstam's canon. (*Toy Story* is also excluded, which seems surprising as the team of odd toys, not least Sid's collection of mutants, may seem perfect examples of Halberstam's alternative group bonding. One must assume that Halberstam regards the toys' loyalty to Andy as too much 'family' ...) (all quotations: Halberstam 2007b).

Family and romance destroy Halberstam's 'Pixarvolt', because they take us into that tale of Oedipus and heteronormativity that queer theory fights.

Halberstam calls for 'non-Oedipal logics', 'new models of generation' which would imply even a new temporality. In the films she celebrates (such as *Finding Nemo*) she finds the 'Oedipal' temporality of continuity, progress and supersession being replaced by 'queer' temporalities of 'the ephemeral, the momentary, the surprise, simultaneity, contradiction, inter-generational exchange' (Halberstam 2007a: 4). Thus she can make an emancipatory hero of the fish Dory suffering from loss of memory (*Finding Nemo*), and celebrate the teenage years of the young birds in *The March of the Penguins* as an emancipatory ideal: 'The young penguins now have five years of freedom, five glorious, non-reproductive, family-free years before they too must undertake the long march' (Halberstam 2007a: 7).

The story and characters of *A Bug's Life* may at a first glance seem to contain Pixarvolt. The circus troupe is certainly a community of odd creatures, and some of them are clearly queer. Not only the male ladybird Francis, who is mistaken for a female by the brute flies and realizes his motherly potential when meeting the ant kids, but also the caterpillar Heimlich (German for 'secret' and 'home-like', but also the positive form of the adjective negated in the Freudian concept of the 'uncanny', 'unheimlich') whose circus acts allude to a non-genital sexuality, as when he presents himself as a nice juicy worm on a stick or does his acts as a giant baby: 'Baby wants pie', perhaps even alluding to the character played by Dennis Hopper in *Blue Velvet*, the pervert sadist Frank, who plays the infant to his victim Dorothy (Isabella Rossellini): 'Baby wants to fuck!' (The name of the grasshopper leader, Hopper, may be an allusion to Dennis Hopper as well, and the kind of sadistic father figure that he plays in *Blue Velvet*.) Despite those odd and queer characters and their successful revolt against oppression, the film can hardly be said to be anti-capitalist, though. The revolt depicted is not a revolt against capitalism, but more like the victory of liberalism over feudalism. In the character of the creative 'bug' Pixar seems to celebrate its own technological innovation.

When the slave becomes the master

In Lacanian terms, the shift from feudalism to capitalism is a shift from the discourse of the master to the discourse of university. Those are two of the, in total, four discourses that Lacan proposes as models of different social bonds. I shall go further into the four discourses in the chapter on *Monsters, Inc.*, so of

U $\quad\quad$ M

$$\frac{S_2}{S_1} \rightarrow \frac{a}{\$} \qquad\qquad \frac{S_1}{\$} \rightarrow \frac{S_2}{a}$$

Figure 5 Lacan's Discourse of the University, Discourse of the Master (Lacan 2007: 29).

interest here will only be the difference between the positions of master and slave in the feudal model (discourse of the master) and in the capitalist one (discourse of the university). Lacan explicitly states that the discourse of the university is the discourse of capitalism (Lacan 2007: 31). It may also be interpreted as the discourse of the slave.

To Lacan, there is discourse as soon as one signifier/position addresses itself to or reaches out for another. In the discourse of the master (M) the master (S_1) addresses himself to the slave (S_2) with the command: Fulfil my desire, which actually also means: Know my desire; Find out what I desire (whereby an object of desire is produced). In the discourse of university (U) the position S_2, which may be understood as the slave, reaches out for the object of desire (*a*), and the master has the position of the hidden truth behind the slave's quest. In one interpretation the discourse of the university/capitalism might as well be called the discourse of the slave, as S_2, which has the defining position in the discourse, is both to be understood as 'knowledge' and as 'slave'.

The idea of the coincidence of slave and knowledge goes back to Hegel. He is the one to state, in *Phenomenology of Spirit*, that the position of the slave is the position of knowledge: the slave is the one who has the know-how, he is the one who develops knowledge and skill in order to fulfil his master's desire. To Hegel, this is why the relationship between master and slave is a dialectical one: through his development of knowledge and skill, the slave will gradually become superior to the master.

In capitalist society the leading position is not held by a master who leaves the work to his servant, but, on the contrary, by a working man who chooses himself what he desires, and goes for it. This is an important and interesting shift in the understanding of being a master. The old master was the one who was liberated from the task of knowing his desire and working; he had people to do that. The new, capitalist master, on the contrary, gains his importance from being busy working (in our society being busy means being important) and has himself the task of knowing and fulfilling his desire. To put it bluntly: the modern capitalist master is a slave, the freedom to choose for yourself what to desire and consume is from another angle a heavy task from which the old master was actually liberated.

The shift from master to capitalist discourse, the moment when the slave becomes the master, is stated by Flik in the scene towards the end when he rises from the dirt and stands up to Hopper: 'Ants are not meant to serve grasshoppers. I've seen these ants do great things. Year after year they somehow manage to pick food for themselves and you. So who is the weaker species? Ants don't serve grasshoppers. It is you who need us.' This is the moment when the slave realizes that through his work he has become superior to his master.

As Hopper is finally conquered, disappearing into a hungry baby bird's beak, the screen goes black (as the camera takes Hopper's point of view). In the next frame the camera movement is reversed: from the inner of a shell, a parallel to the beak, we draw back to the open air, discovering the shell to be a giant wind instrument to an ant accompanying his fellow ants as they are working in the field, carrying harvesting machines invented by Flik. Thus the end of the grasshoppers' regime (feudal society/discourse of the master) and the beginning of the ants' regime (mechanization, liberalism/discourse of university) is pictured as death and rebirth. The master's total black out is preceded by gloomy scenes of rain, storm and war, depicting the end of the grasshoppers' regime as a purifying apocalypse, making way for the new harmonious world of the working ants' society. The fact that it is finally the natural bird that conquers the grasshoppers, and not the artificial one invented by Flik, seems to state the end of their regime as part of the order of nature.

A Bug's Life shows us subjects animated by the pun, society animated by the dialectics of master and slave, progress animated by creative experiments and mistakes, social subversion animated by multiplication, and entertainment as warfare. As usual there is a certain amount of self-celebration in these themes: puns, entertainment, creative mistakes, and the technique of multiplication are important dimensions of Pixar's own work.

5

There is Nothing More Toxic than a Human Child: *Monsters, Inc.*

'The question is not: Why does the Matrix need our energy. The question is: Why does our energy need the Matrix?' Thus Slavoj Žižek in *The Pervert's Guide to Cinema* about the 'matrix' feeding on energy from human beings in the famous sci-fi films by the Wachowski brothers.

Žižek's point is that 'our libido needs illusion in order to sustain itself', that our drive feeds on fantasy images, the filmic fantasy about a 'matrix' feeding on human energy being one example of such an image.

Watching *Monsters, Inc.* (Pete Docter, David Silverman, Lee Unkrich, 2001), Pixar's fantasy about a society of monsters dependent on energy from scared human children, one is tempted to take over Žižek's reversal: The question is not: Why do monsters need the energy of children, but rather: Why does the energy of children (and animators) need monsters?

The film revolves around the company 'Monsters, Inc.' which supplies the monsters' (quite NY-like) society Monstropolis with energy by extracting screams from children in their bedrooms. The company has a kind of 1920s cooperative spirit about it: nice monster guys working hard, proudly serving the company and thereby society. (The 1920s ambience is suggested also by Randy Newman's cheerful music hall music.) Being the most productive worker, that is the one who has extracted the most and loudest screams, is a matter of honour. The position is held by the big, hairy, blue-and-green monster Sully (John Goodman) who is the film's protagonist, almost always in company with his small friend Mike (Billy Crystal), truly an oddball, looking like a walking green testicle with one big eye. The technique of scream extraction consists in the monster being presented to one door after the other suspended in the great working hall, entering it and accessing the bedroom of a human child, making it scream and thereby produce the energy which is then collected in the company's supply system. From the perspective of the monsters, the child is scary and contagious. As pronounced by the head of company, the giant crab spider

Figure 6 Boo and Sully. The toxic human child. From *Monsters, Inc.* (Pete Docter, 2001) © Pixar.

Waternoose (James Coburn): 'There is nothing more toxic, nothing more deathly than a human child.' It suffices that a child's sock gets attached to a monster and taken into the monsters' world for the disinfection troops to take action. Now, suddenly Sully finds himself with a human girl on the wrong side of the door: the small and unscared Boo (Mary Gibbs) has slipped into the monsters' world, finding Sully kind of cute. While Sully and Mike are trying to bring Boo back to her bedroom, they discover an ongoing intrigue in the company: their boss Waternoose and their chameleonic colleague Randall (Steve Buscemi) working on a new machine to extract screams directly and violently from the mouths of children. After much chasing in the corridors and searching behind the freely suspended doors (opening to different parts of the world) Boo is finally brought back where she belongs, and Waternoose and Randall revealed as evil traitors. By the presence of Boo, Mike and Sully have accidentally discovered children's laughter to be an even more powerful source of energy than their screams, so now all monsters are retrained into comedians as their job is not any longer to make the children scream, but to make them laugh. Sully is promoted to lead the energy extraction, but he is not really happy, missing Boo. In the final scene Mike has succeeded in restoring Boo's maculated door, Sully enters, and Boo happily addresses him from her bed: 'Kitty?'

Pixarvolt

Does this sound queer? The film has indeed attracted attention from queer theorists, Judith Halberstam enrolling it in her canon of animated films containing 'Pixarvolt' (Halberstam 2007b, cf. this book Chapter 4), and Elisabeth Freeman considering Boo and Sulley's attachment to be 'dangerously queer: cross-generational and cross-species' (Freeman 2005: 89).

Halberstam does not go into an analysis of *Monsters, Inc.*, but the film's alliances, between a hairy monster and a walking eyeball, and between a monster and a small girl, seem to match perfectly her call for queer, cross-generational and cross-species alliances between odd creatures coming together to oppose exploitation, here the evil-exploiting forces ready to use any means to sustain the energy consumption of a rich society. Halberstam might feel, though, the love story between Mike and his girlfriend to threaten the Pixarvolt. Even if Mike is a walking testicle, and his girlfriend is a one-eyed Medusa with snakes for hair, I do not think this would save them from being accused of heteronormativity. On the contrary one might see Mr Testicle and Miss Medusa as emblematic for the positions of 'man' and 'woman' in patriarchy. Only I would tend to see them also as an emblem of the very 'queerness' of the hetero, of the idea, contrary to what queer theory believes, that the relationship between man and woman might be the most queer of all relationships.

A crisis of transference

Also from a queer perspective, but arguing by way of the psychoanalytic concepts of desire and transference, Elisabeth Freeman does unfold a thorough and interesting analysis of *Monsters, Inc.* Freeman reads the film as an allegory of the institutions of education, as she interprets the extraction of energy from the children as an image of that energy the system of education has to produce in order to make society function (Freeman 2005: 87). Freeman draws our attention to the libidinal character of that energy, the importance in the student–teacher relationship of what psychoanalysis calls 'transference', that is libidinal investment in an impersonal relationship (such as that between client and shrink). In *Monsters, Inc.* she sees the relationship between scaring monster and screaming child as an allegory of that transference, but she also sees 'the monster' as an allegory of transference itself. The idea of extracting energy directly and violently from the children is seen by Freeman as the current tendency of education to repress transference and desire as its important components.

According to Freeman (2005), *Monsters, Inc.* is 'a story about class and class rooms' (85), and about 'the impact of new technologies on intergenerational encounters' (86). Her thesis that this is a film about education was actually strengthened by the release of the prequel *Monsters University* (Dan Scanlon, 2013), which seems to combine *Animal House* and *Harry Potter* in the story of Mike and Sully as freshmen.

Freeman understands the crisis of energy in Monstropolis as a crisis of transference (Waternoose: 'Children do not get scared the way they used to') and the direct and painful extraction of energy from the children as an 'oral violation' (2005: 90) dismissing transference and desire as components of education. (The interpretation of the extraction machine as performing some kind of oral violation could be heavily supported by the vaginally swollen lips of Waternoose's helper who lands in the machine instead of Boo.)

One might transfer this logic into the field of psychotherapy, regarding the extraction machine as an allegory of the cognitive or medical treatment of clients, fixing the 'problem' mechanically and directly, as opposed to psychoanalysis which works through desire and transference, that is through staging some kind of psychodrama between analyst and analysand, just as a psychodrama is staged between child and monster in *Monsters, Inc.*

Freeman is not satisfied with the end of the film, though. Making the children laugh may be a better alternative to the oral violation of the extraction machine, but according to Freeman it only reflects what is happening in late capitalism: scream has turned into laughter as 'symbolic manipulation' has replaced violent force, and the production of surplus (branding) value has become more important than hard physical labour, making 'profiteering look like participatory fun' (2005: 91).

Thus expanding her interpretation not only to the educational but to the whole capitalist system, Freeman regards the children's bodies as representing the exploited (and hidden) bodies of capitalism – Boo then being 'the exploited raw material making itself visible' like a 'student activist', manifesting 'pure id' (2005: 88).

Here the connection between 'student activist' and 'pure id' is not very clear. To read activism into the character of Boo is certainly an interpretative choice, whereas her id quality is barely to be ignored: much like Harpo Marx, who is to Žižek the pure allegory of the id, Boo has this double quality of being truly cute and truly monstrous. Her character may have taken much inspiration from the girls in the animation films by Miyazaki (acknowledged by Pixar as a great source of inspiration): the baby sister in *Totoro* and Ponyo in *Ponyo* for instance who like Boo incarnate some completely fearless, uninhibited girl power, admirable, lovable as well as truly annoying.

It is interesting that Boo should be named after that call of the monsters supposed to scare her ('Boo!'), the scary exclamation turning into a vocative: *Boo! Boo? I wanted to scare you by my call, but as it didn't scare you it became your name*... The name of Sully seems to have a similar dialectics in it – in a Freudian slip Freeman writes that 'Sully's job' is to 'eliminate the unruly body that might *sully* the pedagogical encounter' (Freeman 2005: 89, my italics), thus making us see that Sully actually carries as his name the predicate of that object (abject) he is meant to keep at a distance.

Whereas Halberstam's 'Pixarvolt', though I really do like the concept and would like to adopt it for my own purposes, is to me an example of queer theory celebrating anything beyond Oedipus, or actually celebrating that kind of teenage society in which we are living, dismissing the sexual and generational division (Lacan's 'symbolic castration'), Freeman's analysis is more thorough and complex, insisting that desire and transference are and should be at work in human relations generally, and educational relations specifically. Leaning on Lacan's definition of the four discourses in seminar XVII, one might say that Freeman opts for a re-hysterization of the university discourse.

The discourses

Lacan's discourses are models of social bonds. They are defined by four positions: (1) the agent acting upon or addressing itself to (2) the other one, producing a (3) product and being driven by (4) some repressed or unacknowledged 'truth'. In these four positions Lacan lets circulate four signifiers: S_1 (the master or simply the first signifier); S_2 (the slave, which is also the place of knowledge, or simply the second signifier); *a* (the object of desire); and $ (the hysterical subject).

$$\overset{U}{\frac{S_2}{S_1} \rightarrow \frac{a}{\$}} \qquad \overset{M}{\frac{S_1}{\$} \rightarrow \frac{S_2}{a}} \qquad \overset{H}{\frac{\$}{a} \rightarrow \frac{S_1}{S_2}} \qquad \overset{A}{\frac{a}{S_2} \rightarrow \frac{\$}{S_1}}$$

Figure 7 Lacan's four discourses (Lacan 2007: 29).

Each of the discourses takes its name from that signifier which is in the position of the agent. S_2: the university discourse (U) (as S_2 signifies the knowledge of the slave); S_1: the master's discourse (M); $\$$: the hysterical discourse (H); *a*: the analytical discourse (A) (as the analyst has to pose in the function of *a*: the place for projection of the analysand's desire).

The university discourse has 'knowledge' or 'the slave' (or even the slave of knowledge: the scientific or academic researcher) in the position of the agent reaching directly for *objet petit a*. In other words, the discourse believing that the desired object can be reached through accumulation of knowledge. What this discourse produces, though, is the hysterical or split subject, the very subject of that desire which can never be fulfilled, and certainly not through accumulation of knowledge. The 'truth' of the university discourse is 'the master': the ideological values or economic interests that decide what kind of knowledge is being accumulated, and what kind of object is to be reached for, even if the university researcher will believe him- or herself to be working on ideologically neutral, scientific grounds. It is this kind of discourse that Freeman sees and criticizes in the educational system, finding an allegory for it in the machine (the slave) sucking out energy (*petit a*) directly from children.

Now, interestingly Lacan sees the capitalist discourse as an instance of the university discourse. That is, capitalist society is built upon the belief that object *a* can be reached, desire can be fulfilled, through hard work, including scientific and technical development. Whereas feudal society would put the master in the first position of the discourse, addressing the slave to fulfil his needs and know his desire (even better than himself), the 'master' of capitalist society is actually the slave: the hard-working, self-made man. In feudal society privilege would be not to have to work or decide to get one's desire fulfilled (as the slave would do that job for you); in capitalist society privilege is to work and decide for yourself.

In seminar XVII, lecture II, Lacan writes: 'What happens between the classical master's discourse and that of the modern master, whom we call capitalist, is a modification in the place of knowledge' (Lacan 2007: 31). The capitalist era is to Lacan 'the tyranny of knowledge' – 'all-knowing has moved into the place of the master' (32). What has moved into the place of the ancient slave (the one who knew many things, but most of all knew what the master wanted) is 'human material': 'those who are themselves products' (32).

Returning to *Monsters, Inc.* one might see the children in the role of this 'human material', being exploited by Waternoose who would then be in the position of 'the capitalist master'. The 'truth' would be capital or economic interest, driving Waternoose to suck out energy directly from his human material. The split subject or the hysterization produced by this discourse could be observed in the character of Sully, who actually gets attached to a piece of that 'human material' that should be kept invisible in the system, which finally makes him defeat his master.

Love and hysteria

Now, according to Lacan, the discourse in which knowledge is produced is not the university (or capitalist) discourse, but the hysterical one, that is the discourse in which the hysterical, split subject ($) , being driven by desire (*a*) addresses itself at the master (authority, established truth), thereby producing knowledge (S_2). This is what happens for instance when some scholar (say Lacan) invests his libidinous energy in putting his teacher (say Freud or Hegel) in the position of the master, asking him for answers but never being completely satisfied with the responses, thus producing true knowledge. In *Monsters, Inc.* the hysterical discourse could seem to be thus enacted: Boo represents the libidinous energy (*a*) driving Sully ($) to address the system (S_1), producing a revelation of the truth of this system (this revelation being then S_2 = knowledge). Through Sully's encounter with Boo, there is a change from capitalist to hysterical discourse; from knowledge in the position of the master, exploiting directly its human material, to knowledge being produced by the rebel addressing the master – from libidinous energy in the position of the object to be exploited, to libidinous energy in the position of the driving force.

Freeman's point is that this libidinous energy should be recognized as the fuel of education, and even that it has to be embodied – that is, the physical, bodily co-presence of student and teacher, with all those different kinds of desire that it may arouse, does not disturb the process of knowledge, but rather enforces it. (Here one might add that libidinous processes do not only happen between bodies; they might as well go on between, say, a contemporary scholar of literature and a text by William Shakespeare.)

One of Lacan's enigmatic definitions of love is that love is what happens when there is change from one discourse to another. This seems to go for the love story of Boo and Sully, whether one (as above) focuses on the change from capitalist to hysterical discourse, or even detects in the story a change into the analytical discourse. The analytical discourse is the one that has *objet petit a* in the position of the agent, effecting upon 'the other one' a hysterization ($). As some kind of pure libido embodied, Boo could be seen to be this *a* hysterizing Sully.

Seen too much

Leaving the theory of the discourses, there is a remarkable scene in which Boo's gaze clearly has the function of hysterizing or splitting Sully. At a moment Sully accidentally enters into the classroom where Waternoose teaches scaring to monster students, and is asked to demonstrate how to do it. Reluctantly, but professionally, he does his scaring, and his frightening pose is frozen and shown on several monitors, making Boo quiver and cry – and Sully himself despair. This is a kind of dysphoric version of the mirror stage, or the seeing-oneself-on-the-screen, that we saw with Woody in a euphoric version as he watched himself as a TV star. The monitor shows to Sully who he is to the Other – and he does not like what he sees. The scene enters into a theme of 'big O watching you', being suggested already by the logo of the company 'Monsters, Inc.': a capital M with one big eye. If this kind of company surveillance is an instance of the gaze of the Other as the symbolic master, the film also presents us with a well known allegory of the gaze of the Other as the petrifying real: the gaze of the Medusa, in the humoristic version of Mike's girlfriend having staring snakes for hair.

Being to Sully a mirror stage experience (in a version that stresses dis-identification rather than identification), the scene of the monitors is from the child's perspective rather some kind of primal scene (that is, the child's vision of its parents copulating, be it real or fantasized.) Boo witnessing her nice 'Kitty' turning into a scaring monster is not unlike the child realizing that Daddy is not only sweet Daddy, but also does have a violent, aggressive desire – or a desire that at least to the child seems aggressive and violent. The same figure is played through when Waternoose, seemingly the nice paternal authority, turns out to be a villain, accompanied by the spooky chameleon Randall who seems penis-like in his ability to metamorphose. The nice authority has as its shadow the obscene tyrant. And once you have seen this, 'you have seen too much', as Waternoose says to Sully.

An intriguing figure in this context is the character of Roz: a giant female slug, being voiced by a man, the Pixar director Bob Peterson, which adds to her drag-like appearance. Seemingly she is a secretary, a harsh mother figure always scolding Mike for not having filled in his forms, but as the intrigue is revealed she shows herself to be the actual (and benevolent) head of the company, taking over as Waternoose is dismissed. In the constructed failed scenes shown after the end of the film (as this is computer animation, failure has to be constructed), she has a hilarious role of popping up unexpectedly everywhere: from the toilet, from behind the curtain, revealing herself with a heavy, deep laughter (harh-harh-harh). Psychoanalytically, through her gender ambiguity and her always-being-there, she seems to represent some kind of phallic mother: a primal authority, being there before the father.

Having seen too much in *Monsters, Inc.* also implies having been 'backstage'. The film contains a remarkable and suggestive fantasy of 'the world behind' that seems to me to have a certain affinity with a similar fantasy in *Toy Story 2*. In *Monsters, Inc.* the 'world behind', the ontological backstage, is the giant hall where doors are gliding along on suspended transportation lines. The analogy in *Toy Story 2* is the transportation band for luggage in the airport. Telotte, in his book *Animating Space*, notices how the vast warehouse with millions of doors through a combination of subjective and extremely long shots produces 'a dizzying Escher-like vision, where depth disappears' – 'the experience of depth seems a kind of trick produced by flat surfaces' (Telotte 2010: 211). Telotte relates this to a postmodern architecture of 'rhetorical fronts' and 'conventional behinds': the doors as 'the rhetorical front', the children's bedrooms as 'the conventional behind' (211). Thus, to Telotte, the end of the film, Mike staring into the camera and smiling after having opened Boo's reconstructed door, is about regaining Boo, but also about regaining 'a sense of the conventional spatial depth' as Sully's gaze suggests a depth of space, but also relegates this depth off-screen and implies that space is constructed by our point of view (212).

More than to a postmodern architecture of rhetorical fronts, though, I associate the factory hall of sliding doors to the structure of virtual reality. The matrix of the world is no sky of ideas, no phenomenological 'flesh', but rather a moving flatness, a series of surfaces suspended in nothingness, each one containing its own world, its own virtual space. Perhaps this is how the skeleton of the world must look in the time of virtual reality.

The primal scene

The classroom scene of scaring the child who turns out to be a mechanical doll has a certain scary fascination about it. No wonder that the prequel, *Monsters University*, repeats and insists on this scene, making it the climax of the plot, the principal challenge of the characters, Mike and Sully as students, to perform it optimally. Its fascination resides in its quality of the primal scene. It may be a 'child' lying in bed, but the scene seems rather to reflect a child's point of view, an infantile fantasy of finding something strange and mechanical in the bedroom where you expected to find life.

Monsters University opens with a flashback to Mike's childhood when he is on an excursion with his class to the Monsters, Inc. factory and illegitimately sneaks into a child's bedroom with one of the scarers. Here he totally assumes the function of his looks: he is all eye. As an overexcited witness to the strange things going on in the bedroom, he is in the position of the child witnessing the primal scene. At the climax, when the monster roars and the child screams, we have an objective shot of his one big eye, mirroring the erect monster waving his four arms. At the moment of the primal scene he is split in eye and gaze.

Towards the end of *Monsters University*, the scaring scene in the child's bedroom is manifold repeated, as Mike and Sully's team, Oozma Kappa, competes against 'Roar Omega Roar' in scaring a wooden doll in the final round of the university's games. This scaring game seems something like mastering the primal scene. The wooden doll in the bed has the uncanny quality about it that Freud ascribes to the situation where you expect a soul, but find mechanics.

The Oedipal theme is driven to the comical at the end when one member of the Oozma Kappa becomes the boyfriend of another member's mum and has trouble finding the right words: 'Just think of me of your big brother that is marrying your mother', 'We are brothers who share the same mum-slash-wife' . . .

The education of Sully and Mike in *Monsters University* is certainly depicted as that kind of teaching that involves transference, not least through the figure of Mrs Hardscrabble, the distinguished, witch-like myriapod professor. But finally, the university appears as *old school*, old and British like Harry Potter and the accent of Mrs Hardscrabble, voiced by Helen Mirren. Mike and Sully are expelled from university (because of cheating with the measurement of the wooden doll's screams), but work their way up from mailmen to scarers at Monsters, Inc., reflecting the American dream of the self-made man.

The monstrous child

Freeman's interpretation of the children in *Monsters, Inc.* as representing the abused bodies of capitalism has my sympathy. It seems to me, though, that by paying attention to the way the film presents its universe, that is to the fact that we are experiencing the world from the monsters' point of view, we must consider taking seriously the proposal that the actual monsters are the children. What if human children are really monsters? It might be the villain, Waternoose, who pronounces the phrase, 'There is nothing more toxic, nothing more deathly than a human child', but there is a very strong resonance in this sentence from the famous 'Ode to Man' pronounced by the chorus in Sophocles' *Antigone*: 'Nothing is more wondrous than man.' The Greek word translated by 'wondrous' is actually *deinos*, which has the connotation of 'terrible' (as in 'dinosaur'). The resonance of Sophocles' chorus gives to Waternoose's words the weight of an authorial commentary. And who could deny that Waternoose is right when he designates the human species as a murderous one, pointing to the human child and declaring: 'That thing is a killing machine!'

The monstrous, the 'deinos' of humanity would then be what Boo incarnates: the surplus of raw, libidinous energy, be it panic or maniac. This energy is primarily represented by Boo's voice, causing disturbing intensifications of electricity in Monstropolis whenever she is crying or laughing, affirming Žižek's definition of the voice as an 'alien': 'Humanity means: the alien is controlling our human bodies' (*The Pervert's Guide to the Cinema*, Fiennes 2006). The screams and laughter of the children could thus be read as allegories of the voice as this powerful alien defining humanity.

In the film, Monstropolis is the symbolic order (the socio-symbolic world of work and positions and exchange), whereas the human children represent 'the real': that frightful reality behind the separation line (here the doors of children's bedrooms) from which we take our energy.

According to Žižek in *Pervert's Guide*, staring at the cloth waiting for the film to begin is very much like staring into a water closet, waiting for the excrements to reappear. This is what Gene Hackmann is doing as the detective in Coppola's *The Conversation*, and what finally appears is even more abject than excrement: the blood-soiled clothes of a murdered woman. In *Monsters, Inc.*, any leftover from the children is abject, even contagious, if it crosses the border between the ('real') world of the human children and the ('symbolic') world of the monsters.

In a scene reminiscent of the scene from Coppola's *The Conversation*, Sully tries to flush toys from Boo's bedroom down the toilet – only, horrified, to see them reappear in a flood overflowing the basin, as this remainder of 'the real' which cannot be destroyed – the resurrection of the excrement. Later in the film he actually thinks that Boo has been flushed down the toilet, which makes clear how her name is only a 'P' away from being a word for excrement – even if Sully has come to love this excrement . . .

So, what if the human child is really monstrous? Or what if Monstropolis is seen as one large inner landscape being populated by partial objects? (Some of the characters very literally look like partial objects: Mike the wandering testicle, Randall the penis . . .) Then the film could be read as a story of the raw libidinous energy of the id, the panic or maniac surplus represented by the screams and laughter of the children, having to be collected, conserved and reasonably used through the control of the ego. If some of the energy (Boo) is set free, it unsettles his majesty the ego, and the obscene superego (Waternoose/Randall) is activated. Through the defeat of the obscene superego and the expulsion of the surplus of libido, the ego restores the balance of the system, but at a price of a loss to be mourned (Sully mourning the loss of Boo). Through some reparative process, the split subject at the end actually regains access to his lost libido, his piece of the real, but the end is open: what kind of relation can be established to this piece of the real?

Once again reversing the perspective we should finish where we started, at the question: Why do children need monsters? It seems to be clear that the monstrous surplus of energy in children, whether it explodes in screams or laughter, needs to be contained somewhere, for instance in defined images of monsters that will always be easier to cope with (in *Monsters, Inc.* they are even nice guys) than the raw libido of the death drive.

6

'Just Keep Swimming': *Finding Nemo*

Finding Nemo (Andrew Stanton, Lee Unkrich, 2003) tells us the story of the boy clownfish Nemo and his over-protective father Marlin. It is obviously a film about the father–son relationship and presents us with a series of different paternal characters. What stands out in its visual and narrative composition, though, is the theme of the stream. Streams or shoals constantly run through the submarine universe of the film, marking a kind of constant drive forwards. Thus the animating principle here seems to be the stream. In the following I shall focus on the topography of the film, first and foremost on the stream as an allegory of the Freudian drive (which in its purest form is death drive), but also on the recurring containers (places of collecting and rebirth), and on the different zones of the sea as allegories of the symbolic, the imaginary and the real.

Nemo (Alexander Gould) is the only one from a large number of fish eggs to survive, and his mother Coral (Elizabeth Perkins) dies before he is hatched. Marlin (Albert Brooks) becomes the over-protective father, and revolting against this, Nemo, during a school excursion, swims out to touch the bottom of a boat, but is caught by a diver, an Australian dentist, who brings him to his office in Sydney, where Nemo becomes part of a new community: the more or less freaked out fish population in the dentist's fish tank (among them a French cleaning fish called Jacques, and I would so much like to add the family name of Lacan). The leader of the fish tank is the gloomy Moorish idol Gill (Willem Dafoe) who has large scars on his right side. Gill arranges an initiation rite for Nemo who has to swim through 'the ring of fire' (the current of bubbles emanating from the volcano that is a part of the fish tank's decoration), thereby earning the name of 'Shark Bait'. Nemo is meant to be a present for the dentist's niece Darla, a repulsive girl with braces on her teeth, being accompanied by the shower murder music from Hitchcock's *Psycho* as she does her entrance. Through a cunning manoeuvre, involving Nemo swimming through the suction tube to block the filter with a small pebble, the fish soil their tank, forcing the dentist to take them out and put them in plastic bags with water while he is cleaning it.

Nemo's storyline is intercut with that of his father, Marlin, as he swims out to find his son. Marlin soon has the company of the regal blue tang fish Dory (Ellen DeGeneres) who suffers from complete short-term memory loss. Through a series of dangers (sharks, stinging jellyfish, angelfish, being swallowed by a whale) they are helped through the East Australian Current (EAC) by a biker-like and very cool troupe of sea turtles. As they arrive at the dentist's, though, Nemo has succeeded in escaping through the toilet drains ('the porcelain express'), fulfilling what Lacan would call his 'subjective destitution' by taking the position of a piece of shit which is emphasized as we have earlier seen the dentist sitting on the same toilet. Back in the ocean, Marlin resigns and leaves Dory, but Nemo finds her and is reunited with his father. A last dramatic episode occurs (Nemo heroically saving Dory and a whole shoal of fish that have been caught in netting, almost losing his life), before the three of them return to the reef, Marlin now as a self-confident father who is able to let his son free.

This story of finding the balance between protection and freedom presents us with different types of father (the over-protective Marlin, the harsh and mysterious Gill, the sea turtle father, voiced by director Andrew Stanton, who manages to protect his kids and at the same time set them free). We shall look at these father figures through Lacan's distinction between the symbolic and the real father, and his concept of *le nom du père* (the name/no of the father). But first, let us turn to the theme of the stream.

Stream of death, stream of life

The stream may be benign, helping the characters to move on in a euphoric way, as the EAC. But it may also be sinister, as the shoal of grumpy, grey fish being annoyed by Marlin who disturbs their movement. The sinister shoal is reminiscent of urban traffic in the rush hour: masses of people moving one way or the other, seeming to be subjected to some kind of compulsion to repeat rather than on their way to something important. If the grumpy grey fish are on their way for something, it is their death in the fishing nets. Finally the film shows several fish shoals, the movement of which can neither be said to be euphoric nor dysphoric, neither cheerful nor sinister. This is the stream as a kind of neutral inertial drive being its own purpose, just sustaining itself. Thus the figure of the stream can be euphoric, dysphoric, as well as neutral.

Figure 8 Stream of life. From *Finding Nemo* (Andrew Stanton, 2003) © Pixar.

Figure 9 Stream of death. From *Finding Nemo* (Andrew Stanton, 2003) © Pixar.

The character representing the stream as pure momentum is the regal tang fish Dory who suffers from short-term memory loss. She is nothing but momentum; her lack of memory lets her at every moment leave everything behind, and her motto, repeated again and again as a mantra, is 'Just keep swimming!'

As presented in the chapter on *A Bug's Life*, Judith Halberstam makes of Dory a queer emancipatory hero, as her loss of memory releases her from the Oedipal temporality of supersession and connects her to the 'queer' temporality of the ephemeral, the momentary, the surprise (Halberstam 2007a: 4). Also, Halberstam celebrates the friendship between Dory and Marlin as a queer, cross-species alliance, and even suggests that the clownfish as such is a 'queer' fish, because it is actually able to change sex. This may be a biological fact, but is not a theme in the film; it is not a part of the character Marlin. What is a part of his character, though, is his taking on conventionally maternal functions, thus blending into the other cultural gender (rather than another biological sex).

Rather than representing a 'queer' temporality I see Dory as the allegory of Marlin's animating principle, as a principle of pure movement forwards: 'Just keep swimming!' The point that one character can be understood as an element in another character's mind is comically stated when Dory, in the total darkness of the deepest ocean, can only hear Marlin's voice, not see him, and asks: 'Are you my conscience?'

Dory's motto 'Just keep swimming' gathers different meanings throughout the film. In the main plot it represents the golden rule of persevering, insisting, not giving up, that leads Marlin to find what he longs for. But the images of the film offer another interpretation: 'Just keep swimming' might as well be the motto of the inertial and senseless forward movement of the grumpy grey fish, meaning then something like pessimism and resignation: there is nothing to do but just keep swimming, even if it has no sense. Finally, in the scene where Nemo in cooperation with his father liberates the fish caught in the netting, 'keep swimming' becomes the slogan accompanying the rebellion, the imperative to mobilize the collective force of emancipation, as Nemo and Marlin make all the fish keep on swimming downwards until the netting loosens from the ship. The drive (to keep swimming) is staged as a meaningful striving for something (that is, the drive in the service of desire), as a meaningless, inertial drive having no purpose but itself, and as a revolutionary force.

Dory has another insistent line that accompanies her moving on, the address of the dentist: 'P. Sherman, 42 Wallaby Way, Sydney' (which she has read on the diver's mask left behind by the boat that took away Nemo). She repeats it again and again, in a rather annoying way, actually also annoying herself: 'Why do I have to tell you over and over again?' Thus, the line seems to impose itself on Dory as some kind of compulsion to repeat. The fact that Dory is able to remember this line may seem to go against her function as the allegory of pure forward drive without any conscience of the past. But like the inertial drive the line is nothing but its own purposeless dynamics. As Dory keeps repeating it, it is emptied of any sense, does not signify anything. It becomes a chain of pure signifiers, and Dory is condemned to repeat these empty signifiers endlessly.

Thus, the address line points to the same difference in the drive as the motto 'Just keep swimming'. As a signifying line, the address defines the goal of the voyage, the object of the paternal fish's desire, and thereby gives a meaning to the moving on. As a pure chain of signifiers, on the contrary, it shows us the moving on as an empty compulsion to repeat with no purpose but sustaining its own movement.

I would propose the stream or shoal to be an image of that which Freud and Lacan call 'the death drive', or simply 'the drive'.

In his essay 'Beyond the Pleasure Principle', Freud reflects on his observation that the human mind can be ruled by a compulsion to repeat which does not seem to have any purpose or lead to any pleasure. Freud is inspired by, among other things, the shell-shocked soldiers who return from the First World War and keep repeating, in dreams and in thoughts, the explosions that traumatized them. This goes against Freud's own theory that the psychic system has pleasure as its goal. He now realizes that the subject can be driven by forces stronger than the pleasure principle, hence the title of his essay: 'Beyond the Pleasure Principle'. What Freud finds beyond the pleasure principle is some kind of dull and inertial compulsion to repeat. He calls it 'the death drive'. Slavoj Žižek describes it as 'a blind automatism of repetition beyond pleasure-seeking, self-preservation' and declares it to define 'la condition humaine as such' (Žižek 1989: 4–5).

In 'Beyond the Pleasure Principle' Freud also gives examples of repetitions that have a purpose, though. In this essay he tells his famous story of the small child who holds a reel on a string, repeatedly throwing it away while uttering 'o-o-o-o' and drawing it back to himself exclaiming 'da!' (Freud 1955d: 15). With this minimal differentiation between two phonemes ('o' and 'da', interpreted by Freud as 'fort' and 'da') the child is developing a language that can help him to control the separation of which he is normally the passive object. He can himself control when the reel is 'fort' (gone) and when it is 'da' (here), something he cannot do with his primary object, his mother.

In Dory's compulsive utterance, language is not a way of giving meaning to the repetition, though. The address line is rather the chain of signifiers as a senseless compulsion to repeat. That is, until the moment when it suddenly makes sense and actually points out the goal of the voyage. As the chain of signifiers start to signify, to actually refer to something, the death drive, that is the senseless compulsion to repeat, is put in the service of life and desire.

Another forceful image of the senseless current that starts signifying is the shoal of silver-grey fish that circle around Marlin and Dory in the scene where he tries to break up with her ('I do like you, but I do not want to be with you. It is a complicated emotion'). At first the fish are a diffuse crowd in sudden movement, at one moment forming a maelstrom, at the next just a formless mass. But then they gather to form signs, iconically representing the Sydney Opera, indexically forming an arrow, and parodically miming Marlin and his grumpy mood.

Through the euphoric, dysphoric as well as indifferent versions of the stream the film is the story of connecting to and disconnecting from the stream. The story is of the subject being animated by something that in its purest form is a senseless compulsion to repeat, serving the forces of death, but which can also be given sense and made to serve life.

What we are touching upon is the difference between drive and desire. Desire is to Lacan a sliding through the chain of signifiers to reach the object that will never be fully satisfying, but provoke more desire. Furthermore, 'Desire is the desire of the big Other' (Lacan 1979: 235). The big Other, as defined in the chapter on *Toy Story 2*, is 'the subject supposed to know', a position which can be taken by some individualized authority (my father, my teacher, my shrink, my favourite theorist), or be something more abstract: the social and cultural norms, the symbolic order in total.

In the opening of the film Marlin is animated by desire as the desire of the big Other in the sense of a desire dictated by social norms: he poses to the big Other by fulfilling the social expectation of being a good middle-class family man who buys his wife a house (an anemone) with an ocean view in an awesome neighbourhood. The drive that animates Marlin in the quest for his lost son is different from the desire that is dictated by the big Other. It is more inertial, more automatic, more necessary. I figure Dory as an allegory of this kind of desire. There is only one way to go: forwards. Dory reminds us of the dog Lassie (from the film *Lassie Come Home*), which is to Žižek an allegory of the pure drive. The wounded collie who keeps moving on towards her home, not letting anything stop her (Žižek 1997: 81). We are beyond desire, where a dog's gotta do what a dog's gotta do.

To Lacan, the character representing drive beyond desire is not Lassie, but Antigone, the tragic heroine who despite the laws of society insists on burying her dead brother and does not let anything stop her in this project. Antigone acts according to Lacan's ethical axiom: 'Do not give up on your desire' (Lacan 1992: 319–21) which might be another way of saying 'Just keep swimming'. What

Lacan here calls desire is actually what he would elsewhere call drive, as distinct from desire. Or not really distinct, as Lacan actually insists that at its barest, desire is actually (death) drive. The compulsion to repeat and the striving to consume itself are the characteristics of the death drive as well as desire. Drive is a kind of purified desire, desire at its barest, ripped of the words and images that sustain it in the symbolic order. Think of the activity of sex, for instance: ripped of all fantasies and words it is nothing but desire consuming itself in a compulsive-repetitive way. Thus, the purification that takes place in the Greek tragedy ('catharsis') does not to Lacan mean that the subject is purified from desire, but rather that desire is purified into drive.

In *Finding Nemo* the force that animates the subject seems to be the stream that psychoanalysis would call compulsion to repeat, death drive, or merely drive. The inertial moving forwards by compulsion to repeat once again seems to be at stake not only in the theme of the movie, but also as a formal/technical question. The principle of the technique of simulation in computer-animated films is to repeat and multiply a prototypic form in movement. This technique is explained on the extra material of *Finding Nemo* when an animator tells about the difficulties of creating the scene with the many grey fish getting caught in the fishermen's net. The simulation, the principle of repeating the same form in the same movement, caused fish that had escaped from the net to try to enter it again. According to the animator, this would be completely illogical in real life: a fish having escaped would not try to re-enter the net. So there was a conflict between the logic of the technique and the logic of the fish. The question is whether the human logic, the logic of the subject, does not sometimes resemble that of the technique more than that of the fish. Is there not, in the human subject, a dull drive that makes it do things that run against the instinct of self-sustainment? This is the drive that psychoanalysis tries to define by the name of the 'death drive'. As interpreted by Lacan and Žižek, the death drive is not a drive towards death, actually it is a drive that never dies, even if it has to kill the subject. It is a perpetual undying momentum.

According to Lacan, Antigone is 'between two deaths' (Lacan 1992: 243). She is symbolically dead; she is no longer a citizen, as she has been expelled from the state by King Creon. But she is not yet biologically dead. To Lacan, this is exactly the zone in which the tragic hero becomes the subject of a drive beyond desire, and an ethics beyond (social) morality. The ethical hero is on the edge of the symbolic order in which the logic of desire and the morality of society (law) rule.

Marlin and Dory may also be said to be on the edge of the symbolic order, even to die several symbolic deaths or pass through several limbos: the darkness of the deepest sea, the belly of the whale, the anaesthetization of the candy-pink jellyfish, the beak of the pelican, the black outs and white outs that mark on the screen the moments when the protagonists faint.

Sometimes the protagonists seem to be driven towards their temporary deaths by 'death drive' in its more common (and opposite) sense: the temptation to give in, to disconnect from the stream, as when they are attracted to the light of the lantern fish. But the impetus to go on ('Just keep swimming') that may be seen as Lacanian (death) drive, always wins. The film seems to have the point, though, that you must somehow transpose the pure drive (which belongs to the order of the real) into the symbolic order to make it a stream of life, not death. The empty signifiers of Dory's repeated address line must come to signify, to give a sense to the journey. The deathly candy-pink jellyfish must be transformed from lethal monsters into tools of the forward movement, as Marlin makes Dory believe that they are stepping stones in a game of not touching the threads.

A counter image to the forward stream is the circling around in which Marlin and Dory get caught after having left the EAC. They are supposed to swim straight through a kind of misty part of the sea, but find themselves making circles. This circling around is accompanied by Dory's playing games, her endless repetition of the same question to Marlin: 'I am thinking of something and it's small and orange …' and his resigned and repetitive answer: 'It's me.' Dory's question to Marlin resembles the Sphinx's question to Oedipus: 'What walks on four feet in the morning, two in the afternoon and three in the evening?' Oedipus's right answer ('man') is a (tragic) turning point, as it opens his way to Theben where he is to unwittingly marry his mother. Marlin's answer 'me' is, according to Italian philosopher Adriana Cavarero, the answer that Oedipus also ought to have given, recognizing his own singular and not man's general fate in the saying (Cavarero 2000: 7–16). But Marlin's 'me' does not get him anywhere; on the contrary he is caught in endless repetition. This is an echo of an earlier, comical scene in which Marlin is forced to circle around himself when counting his stripes, checking his identity. The subject is referred to nothing but himself, or the imaginary 'me', the image of himself (orange, small, stripes), and this gets him nowhere. What makes the story move on from here is the moment when Dory (Marlin's animating principle) stops just referring him to himself and contacts the whale (the 'Thing') in which the protagonists then get completely blocked, but in a manner preparing for rebirth and further movement.

Containers

The series of temporary deaths in the film is just as well a series of rebirths. Each time Dory and Marlin are trapped in some symbolic grave, they are blown, spat or vomited out again. An especially impressive rebirth happens when the whale sprays out the two fish from its blowhole, almost as if they were two sperms in a forceful ejaculation.

Nemo as well is temporarily trapped several times in some kind of container: the plastic bag in which he is caught by the dentist, the water-filled cooler in which he is put on the boat, the fish tank in the dentist's office. He seems to be reborn several times as well: he slides through the suction tube and swirls through the toilet drain, as if they were birth channels.

Thus, as recurring motifs in the topology of the film, the stream is supplemented by the whirl and by the container, and both have the same ambivalence as the stream: they can be vital and they can be lethal.

The containers can be prisons, but they can also imply the temporary pause and 'collecting oneself' which are necessary to be able to 'keep on swimming'. In this last function they serve as 'containers' in the sense of object relation theory (Bion 1962), that is they have the function of 'containing' (collecting and keeping together) all the different parts and fragments, thoughts and affects, of which the subject consists.

A special container that is a recurring motif in the film is the mouth. The fish enter into different disgusting mouths: the shark's mouth, the whale's mouth, the pelican's beak. But the nastiest mouth is that of man: 'The human mouth is a disgusting place', as one of the fish in the tank says. At the same time the human mouth seems to be an object of fascination to the fish (and to the pelican) who watch the dentist's operations. One might ask why a dentist's office is one of the film's important localities. What does the image of fascinated fish observing patients in the dentist's chair imply? Fish regarding the pain of others? The dentist's chair is one of the places where we get close to the real at the core of human existence, the pain beyond symbolizations and constructions, the fact that in our innermost we consist of skulls and bones that are to survive us. As part of the decoration of the fish tank, there is an actual skull, serving as Gill's house. At the moment when the fish at the dentist's have lost hope, there is an image juxtaposing the skull and its teeth to Darla's teeth behind the broken glass of the picture frame, thus connecting teeth with death. Right after, we share Gill's point of view, looking out on Nemo through the skull's open eye hole. Here our point of view is literarily framed by death.

The fish tank is like the sea enclosed in a container, which is effectively shown from Nemo's point of view as he wakes up and bumps into the transparent walls of the tank. If you are watching the movie on your TV, the tank seems a replication of the TV box or screen. As if we had ourselves entered the TV, as we share the point of view of the fish in the box. This brings us to a fourth recurring figure in the topology of the film: inversion. The start of the film cuts from the small quivering red spot of life, Nemo before his birth, to a vibrating light reflection in the surface of the sea. At first you may think it to be the reflection of the moon in the water, as seen from above, from a normal human point of view. But in the following movement of the camera you learn that it is the reflection of the sun in the water, seen from beneath. Here the surface of the sea is the horizontal axis of inversion.

The real and the Thing

Besides the stream, the containers and inversion, the characteristic thing about the topography of the film is the division of the sea into a colourful universe of light on the one side, and an amorphous grey world on the other. Visually the film succeeds in creating a paradise version of the submarine world, reminiscent of Hans Christian Andersen's 'The Little Mermaid' (2004). The colourful zones of the sea make a kingdom of light, light, light. On the commentary track you can hear the animators tell how they have worked hard to produce the special quality of light characteristic of fish. As art director Robin Cooper explains, they had to work with 'several layers of light' to create the 'look' that differentiates fish from plastic. Fish are creatures of light, a bit like angels, but in Pixar's intern terminology they are compared to gummy bears. Director Andrew Stanton tells us that they actually lacked a name for the special light effect they were striving to produce, but then someone came up with the gummy bear metaphor: the more gummy bear, the better . . .

In Lacan's terms the colourful light world is a symbolic-imaginary universe, while the grey, formless sea is a vision of the real. As explained in the chapter on *Toy Story 2*, the symbolic order is the differentiating order of language, desire and social positions, the imaginary order is the order of complete and clearly defined figures, while the real is that which has no differentiation or figure, such as flesh and the song of the sirens. In *Looking Awry*, Slavoj Žižek explains the real by an image taken from Robert Heinlein's science fiction novel *The Unpleasant*

Profession of Jonathan Hoag, in which our world is revealed to be just one among different worlds created by mysterious creatures. The protagonist and his wife are contacted by one of those creatures who informs them that some minor defects in the universe have to be repaired, so when they are driving through the city, they should not open the window of their car. As, from the car, they witness an accident on the street, they cannot help scrolling down the windowpane, only to find that all people and objects have disappeared, outside there is 'nothing but a grey and formless mist, pulsing slowly as if with inchoate life' (Žižek 1991: 14). To Žižek, this grey and formless mist is an allegory of the real, while the car and its windowpane are an allegory of the symbolic. Translated into the images of *Finding Nemo*: as long as the submarine world has clear colours and figures we are in a kind of aquarium, behind a screen, the screen and aquarium of the categories by which we make sense of the world. Outside this aquarium there is nothing but a grey and formless sea.

Another image of the border between the real and the symbolic/imaginary is the scene with the seagulls that get stuck with their beaks in the sail as they are after Nemo and Dory. The seagulls are a humorous reference to Hitchcock's *The Birds* – at first they appear silent and threatening, gathered by numbers in the masts around Dory, Marlin and the pelican, just as the birds silently gather in stands and telephone wires around the heroine of Hitchcock's film.

The seagulls are pictured as driven by primitive impulse, egoistically and by reflex fixated on the object to fulfil their need. They have some kind of language, but their language has one element, one syllable ('Mine! Mine! Mine!'), thus they are not thrown into the differentiating principle of human language. Just like Hitchcock's birds they seem to represent something presymbolic that is then kept out from symbolic-imaginary reality through the sail in which their beaks get stuck.

The seagulls' stupidity and fixation on satisfying their need do make them far less scary than Hitchcock's birds, though. They want something definite, which Hitchcock's birds do not. Hitchcock's birds are like stains on the cinema cloth. Nobody knows where they come from or what they want. They are the stain, originally a negative entity in the image, made into a motif, that is, a positive entity. Hitchcock's birds come close to presenting the real (the stain, the negativity with no meaning or purpose), whereas the seagulls in *Finding Nemo* represent it in a light and humorous way.

Nemo's story begins at the frontier between the symbolic/imaginary and the real. This frontier is clearly marked as the frontier between the reef and the abyss of the grey, amorphous sea. In the element of the real is a big, grey, silent, resting object: the boat. Later in the film the boat has a parallel in the body of the whale, also a big, grey object resting in the grey. The body of the whale is accompanied by whale song – a kind of primal sound before or beyond articulation, comparable to the soundtrack in David Lynch's *The Elephant Man* that Žižek characterizes by Michel Chion's term 'le rendu' ('the rendered'): 'a pulse that does not imitate or symbolize anything, but that seizes us immediately, "renders" immediately the thing'. To Žižek, this kind of sound is the sound of the real: 'the beat of that "grey and formless mist, pulsing slowly as if with inchoate life"' (Žižek 1991: 41).

The boat and the body of the whale are instances of that which Lacan, picking a term from Freud's 'Project for a Scientific Psychology', calls 'la Chose', 'the Thing', in German: 'Das Ding' (Lacan 1992: 43–70). The element of the Thing is the real; it belongs to the realm of that which has no name or figure. The Thing is presymbolic; its prototype is the prelinguistic maternal body, the idea of a maternal body being there before language.

In the plot of the film a maternal body actually disappears in the beginning, Nemo's mother Coral who dies before he is born. But the maternal body returns, as boat and as whale, in the guise of the ambivalent Thing, attractive and scary at once.

Žižek defines the Thing as 'some strange, traumatic element which cannot be symbolized, integrated into the symbolic order (but at the same time is at the center of symbolic order)' (Žižek 1989: 132). Its site is 'between two deaths' (135), its place is 'the sacred/forbidden, empty place in the Other' (195). Nemo ventures into this place as he leaves the clear colours of the reef to go for the boat-Thing in the grey sea.

Lacan connects the Thing to the sublime Object. He combines Freud's idea of 'sublimation' with Kant's idea of 'the sublime' ('das Erhabene') as that which gives us aesthetic pleasure through exceeding the forms and categories by which we usually make sense of the world (in Lacanian: through exceeding the symbolic order). Sublimation, with Lacan, is not replacing sex by some other activity, but replacing the (impossible) Thing by some real object. To Žižek, this is why the wreck of *Titanic* is sublime. The ship of luxury and enjoyment, the huge and lost object at the bottom of the sea, is a stand-in for the lost Thing, the lost maternal body. In *Finding Nemo*, wrecks, whales and boats are exactly Things situated in the zone of the real, the deepest and greyest zone of the sea.

The diver from the boat-Thing is masked and breathing heavily like some kind of Darth Vader, some kind of primal father. The primal father also belongs to the presymbolic zone. He is the father before or beyond the symbolic father, before or beyond the paternal authority who communicates language and social order. The diver loses his mask, which then becomes a kind of independent partial object, a kind of object-gaze detached from its body. The detached partial object again situates us in the zone of the real of the drive. The real of the drive can be figured as the partial object that has a life of its own, like 'The Red Shoes' that carry away the girl in Hans Christian Andersen's tale and continue dancing with her feet still in them, even after those have been cut off: 'These shoes stand for drive at its purest, an "undead" partial object that functions as an impersonal kind of willing – "it wants", it persists in its repetitive movement (of dancing), it follows its path and exacts its satisfaction at any price, irrespective of the subject's well-being' (Žižek 1997: 81).

Names of the father

So Nemo gets in touch with the real, he gets close to the Thing. From that point on his story is the story of re-entering (properly entering) the symbolic order. In Lacan's terms the subject enters the symbolic order through symbolic castration. 'Castration' is here in itself to be understood symbolically, as a metaphoric cut in the little amorphous lump of human flesh, a cut separating the subject from its symbiosis with the object (psychogenetically speaking the maternal body) and creating a split in the subject itself. Entering into the symbolic order, the order of desire and language, is to be separated and split. The symbolic castration is a cut that in one movement separates mother and infant, word and thing, desire and object, the conscious from the unconscious, and sends out the split subject on the track of language and desire.

The moment of the symbolic castration is also the moment of the interpellation, the giving of a name (this theoretical idea seems concretized in the Jewish rite of circumcision and name-giving in one). To give a name to the subject, to mark it by a signifier, is to inscribe it in the social and linguistic (the symbolic) order, thus symbolically castrating it. The coincidence of naming and symbolic castration is expressed in Lacan's pun 'le nom du père' which means 'the name of the father', but in French sounds exactly like 'the no of the father': 'le non du père'.

Nemo at first is given his name at the moment of his birth, being in his case a radical separation from the maternal body that dies and disappears. He starts as a small quivering lump of red jelly, but becomes a subject the moment his father calls him by his name: Nemo. This name is presented as the unique mark that separates itself from Marlin's idea that all his baby fish boys should be called Marlin, and all his baby fish girls Coral. Nemo is given a unique identity by his name, which turns him into a being of the signifier, a linguistic being, a *parlêtre* as Lacan calls the human subject as distinct from the animal. The name 'Nemo' is Coral's idea and thus a sign of the mother's desire and the father's desire to keep alive the mother's desire. The name becomes a symptom, understood as the symptom of the Other's (the parents') desire. This is generally true of the names that we carry; they are expressions of our parents' desire (wishes and visions for our lives).

In the fish tank Nemo is given a name a second time, by a second paternal figure. He goes through an initiation rite in which he has to jump through 'the ring of fire', thereby earning the name of 'Shark Bait', given to him by the grim leader Gill. 'Shark Bait' is an ambiguous name: it is given to Nemo as a sign of honour, celebrating his courage and strength, but semantically it marks him as weak and fragile, potentially shark food. This ambiguity is characteristic of the symbolic castration: to be inscribed into the symbolic order is to have a position, but it is also to be inscribed into finality, contingency and mortality, to be separated and split.

Gill is an alternative paternal figure to Marlin; he is the grim, slightly scary father who turns out to be good to the son exactly by being grim. He performs the symbolic castration in which Marlin, suffering from separation anxiety, has not really succeeded. Gill himself visually has a symbolic mark of castration: the large scars on his right side. At the beginning of the initiation rite, when we share Nemo's point of view, swimming towards the volcano in the nightly darkness of the fish tank, Gill appears above the volcano, in an elevated position like some tribal chief, and we only see his left side, the side with no scars. Thus he appears as the 'uncastrated' paternal figure that Freud and Lacan call 'the primal father', the fantasy of an omnipotent paternal figure who is not himself subjected to the symbolic castration to which he subjects others. Freud's allegory is the leader of the primal tribe who could eat, fornicate and kill as he wanted, thus not being subjected to the taboos and interdictions that he imposed on his sons (Freud 1955a). The fact that Gill's voice is Willem Defoe's emphasizes this state. Willem Defoe is often cast as some kind of primal father (the brute, reckless villain, taking enjoyment from his cruel deeds), and when Žižek in *The Pervert's Guide to Cinema* wants to explain the figure of the primal father, his primary example is Willem Defoe in the role of the sadistic psychopath Bobby Peru in David Lynch's *Wild at*

Heart. As soon as the initiation rite is completed, Nemo courageously having traversed the bubbling current emanating from the volcano, we see Gill from his wounded side, reminding us that even the father is symbolically castrated, even he is split and desiring, the fantasy of some uncastrated omnipotent position of full and constant satisfaction is just a fantasy. To Lacan, it is part of the subject's symbolic castration to realize that even the father is symbolically castrated. Thus Gill's two sides, the one without and the one with scars, might be said to represent the two sides of the paternal figure: the uncastrated primal father, and the castrated symbolic one.

The primal father also appears in the guise of another character in the film: the dentist's niece, the monster child Darla. She enters into the office accompanied by the sound that has become the very sign of the psychopath: the sound accompanying the knife murder in the shower scene from Hitchcock's *Psycho*. Showing her teeth, which through their braces monstrously seem to transgress the border between human material and metal, she seems related to yet other primal paternal figures in the film, the sharks. Just as Lacan says that one of the names of the primal father is 'Woman', one might say that one of his names is 'child'. The fantasy of a monstrous, uncastrated creature that has no other intention than maximizing its own enjoyment applies in our culture to women as well as children. The child (notably the female child) as monster is a recurring figure in Pixar, most notably in *Monsters, Inc*. The photo of Darla is marked by a fissure in the glass. This does not give the impression of a castration mark, though, rather it appears as a sign of the monster child's destructive force, emanating even from her photo.

Apart from Gill's scars there are other symbolic marks of castration in the film: the meeting with the candy-pink jellyfish leaves Dory with a wound, and Nemo has one fin that is smaller than the other. Nemo's father has taught him to call the small fin his 'lucky fin', thereby transforming a deformity into something productive by giving it a name, which is perhaps exactly what symbolic castration does: it handicaps the subject by cutting into any illusion of unity and perfection, but at the same time this cut is what sets the subject on the track of language and desire.

Not only Nemo is given different names, so is his father. He is called Marlin, he is called Dad, he is called Clownfish, and he is called Jellyman. As a character he is suspended between the name 'Clownfish', the fish supposed to be funny, and the name 'Jellyman', which interpellates him as an epic hero, the one who survived swimming through the jellyfish. 'Clownfish' is an example of the name as a symptom of the big Other's desire, a name that raises the others' expectations as expressed by the other fish fathers at the school: 'Tell us a joke, Clownfish!'

Marlin is not capable of satisfying this demand until the end of the film when he returns from his great quest and finally succeeds in making the others laugh. In this story of fitting into his name, Marlin's story is following the track of desire rather than the track of drive: he finally delivers that which the big Other wants from him. The word 'deliver' is the one he uses himself in the beginning when, having fulfilled the ideal of the middle-class family man, he says 'Did your man deliver?' to Coral when showing her their new home. In one of the outtakes to be watched in the bonus material, Marlin has this point about the good joke: 'It's all in the delivery.' The story of Marlin as a man who finally delivers what the others (the Other) want from him, is to me less heroic than the story of Marlin as a man who lets himself be led by pure drive.

Part of the theme of names is Dory's forgetting of names. She does not remember any names, but constantly invents new ones – even at the end of the film when she calls Nemo 'Elmo'. Compared with the burden of carrying a name as a symptom of the big Other's desire there is a certain liberation in sending off the name in a sliding chain of signifiers, as does Dory. Also this makes her a figure of free mobility, unbound by the past. The deference of names points to that which can set free the subject: to throw itself into the stream of signifiers in a playful and productive way, instead of being subjected to them as a compulsion to repeat.

Beside Gill and Marlin there is a third father figure in the film, the sea turtle Crush. He is voiced by the director of the film, Andrew Stanton, and there are indications that he represents the director's idea of an ideal father. On the commentary track Stanton tells that he had the idea for the film because he was wondering how to be a good father. He tells of an episode when he was taking a walk with his 5-year-old son and found himself being too busy telling him to be careful instead of just enjoying walking with him. In the film Crush is the paternal figure who seems to manage the equilibrium between taking care of and challenging his sons. Giving them 'optimal' (not maximal) frustration (Heinz Kohut's term for the parents leaving the child so much on his own that he gradually learns to take care of himself, but no so much that he breaks (Kohut 1971: 64)). It does get a little ironic that a sea turtle has this ideal paternal role. Crush proudly tells about just leaving his small kids on the beach, and then they will find their way out in the ocean all by themselves. In reality the story of the small self-hatched baby turtles wandering towards the ocean is one of nature's most cruel stories, a total massacre in which only one out of every thousand survives the attacks of the hungry crabs and birds.

As a parent it is difficult not to be moved to tears by the successful relationships between fathers and sons in the film (thus fulfilling the intention of director Stanton: 'I wanted to make it so that by the end of the movie, every male in the audience would have no choice but to cry' (Paik 2007: 212)). But here one could take a warning from the image of the sentimental sharks that Dory and Marlin meet on their voyage. The sharks are hilariously staged as some kind of AA members, fish addicts trying to leave their addiction behind. In the film they are the ones to shed tears over Marlin's love and longing for his son. The image of the sentimental shark points to a certain familiarity between sentimentality and brutality. The one who is sentimentally enjoying his own emotion is thereby able to avoid real feelings and empathy.

The film's story of becoming the ideal father is finally a story about 'delivering', satisfying the big Other's desire, including the spectator's desire to be sentimentally touched. But the way that leads to this end tells a story about the (death) drive as the animating human principle, and how it can be transformed from a compulsive inertia into a productive stream of signifiers, just as Dory's senseless repetition of the same syllables suddenly gives directions, or her monotonous refrain 'Just keep swimming' suddenly accompanies the rebellion of the exploited.

7

More than Super: *The Incredibles*

The Incredibles (Brad Bird, 2004) tells the story of a family of superheroes living undercover in a 1950s-style American middle-class suburb. In the figure of the superhero the animating principle becomes each hero's specific superpower, or, as Lacan would put it: 'that-which-is-in-you-more-than-yourself'. As we shall see, this 'more' is depicted in several ways: as monstrous excess, as imaginary identity, as a signifier, as the repressed superpower of the family man as well as the family power demanded of the domesticated superman. The family of superheroes having to hide away their special powers and live as a normal American middle-class family come to represent an immanent aporia of democracy: how do we unite the principle of equality with the principle of unique individuality?

The film opens with the superhero characters presenting themselves one by one, staged as in a kind of talk show, addressing themselves directly to the camera, the images and framing imitating that of television in its early days. We are introduced to Mr Incredible (Craig T. Nelson; incredibly strong), Elastigirl (Holly Hunter; super-flexible) and Frozone (Lucius Best; able to produce ice and skate it everywhere, combining the magical talent of the twentieth-century superhero with the Afro-American coolness of twenty-first-century street style). We then see Mr Incredible in his car, driving the streets of an American city having the qualities of a city in a computer game. He is (as we will later learn) heading for his wedding with Elastigirl, but has the time to do a few jobs on the way: saving a cat, catching a robber on a roof (in erotically rivalling cooperation with Elastigirl), catching a suicidal man jumping from the top of a building, dealing with the French bomb man Bomb Voyage, stopping a train from falling into the abyss of a broken track. During those incidents he is annoyed by his 'number one fan' who calls himself 'Incrediboy' (Jason Lee) and imitates Mr Incredible's superpowers by means of his own technical inventions. Mr Incredible rejects 'Incrediboy': 'Fly home, Buddy, I work alone.'

After Mr Incredible's and Elastigirl's wedding, the superheroes get into hard times. In the style of a news report from the 1950s we learn how the public does not want them any more. Mr Incredible is taken to court by the man whom he saved from suicide: 'You didn't save my life, you ruined my death.' Newspaper pictures show how clumsy superhero life-size dolls are publicly burned, like effigies of presidents, and how superhero statues are torn down, like the statues of dictators. The news-reporting voice informs us that the superheroes are now living among us as 'average citizens, average heroes, quietly and anonymously continuing to make the world a better place', and then there is an ironic cut to Mr Incredible in a shirt '15 years later', sad and resigned in his tiny office at the insurance company, staged as a grey and bureaucratic hell of straight lines and uniformity. He and Elastigirl are now living undercover in a modernist 1950s-style middle-class suburb as Bob and Helen Parr with their three children.

We get the picture of a man unhappily trapped in his life as a family father and working man, longing for his glory days. His being trapped is visually communicated in his being far too large for his tiny office and his tiny car. Sick and tired with 'celebrating mediocrity', as he puts it when not wanting to go to a ceremony at his son's school, he finds a little release in going out with Frozone, listening to police scanners and seeking out fires and crimes to save people, doing 'moonlighting hero work', as the designer Edna later puts it. Helen (Elastigirl) is more committed to her new life as a housewife, working hard to hold together the family and hide their super identity, including the children's superpowers: the teenage daughter Violet has the power to make herself invisible and produce protective force fields, her younger brother Dash runs incredibly fast, and the baby Jack-Jack will at the end of the film reveal himself as a monster baby able to transform himself into fire.

As Bob (Mr Incredible) is called to see his boss (a tiny, choleric little man, whose contrast to his employee's large body emphasizes a modern power relationship that has nothing to do with physical strength) and told off because he helps his clients (and not the stockholders); he cannot control himself any more, but throws his boss through several walls and is fired. At the same time he is contacted by the secret agent Mirage (Elizabeth Peña) who wants his help to destroy a robot that has taken control of itself on the 'Nomanisan Island' ('No man is an island'). This leads him (and us) to the film's other universe: a very James Bond-like high-tech base situated on a tropical island with jungle plants, caves and waterfalls. It will turn out that this world is created by Incrediboy, now calling himself Syndrome, planning to destroy Mr Incredible and become himself the new celebrated superhero.

Even if Mr Incredible suffers from being an ageing, middle-class father (too fat, back problems), he succeeds in destroying the robot (by getting into it, thus making it turn its aggression towards itself), and as he returns, a period of happy family life begins, told in images of Mr Incredible exercising (that is, lifting train wagons and that kind of thing), playing with his children, flirting with his wife, leaving home and coming back in his new sports car. He seems at once to fulfil his roles as a working man, a caring father and a loving husband perfectly. As he is called to Nomanisan Island once again, telling his wife that he is going on a business trip, she starts suspecting him of having an affair as she has heard Mirage's female voice speaking to him on the phone. Through the designer Edna (a hilarious, tiny figure, meant to appear half-German, half-Japanese, voiced by director Brad Bird) and by the means of an electronic device installed in his new suit, she situates his location and takes off in a jet plane to join him, finding that Dash and Violet (suspecting that their parents' life, 'or worse: their marriage' is in danger) have sneaked into the plane with her. As the plane is attacked and explodes, she gets her children safely to the island by forming first a parachute, then a boat, out of her hyper-flexible maternal body.

Meanwhile, revealed by his beeper at his wife's call, Mr Incredible has been captured by Syndrome and suspended like a mixture of the crucified Jesus and da Vinci's Vitruvian Man in an electronic torture machine (this image is actually prefigured by the images of Mr Incredible exercising, suspended by wires between wagons, thus suggesting an analogy between suffering on the cross and suffering in the fitness centre). Through a series of intrigues and scenes of chase, in which all members of the super-family finally get to use (and in the children's case: discover) their superpowers, they are united and manage to escape the island, getting to Metroville just in time to destroy the robot that Syndrome has planted in order to defeat it and become the new celebrated superhero himself. On their way home, escorted by the (this time grateful) government official who takes care of their allocation, Helen listens to the telephone messages of Jack-Jack's babysitter, still more desperate about the baby's special behaviour, and at home they find Jack-Jack in the arms of Syndrome who is finally vanquished by the baby himself, transforming into fire and devils as Syndrome tries to fly him to his plane, in the propeller of which the villain (fulfilling a trace laid out by designer Edna's stories of superheroes killed by their cape) finally gets stuck and dies. In the epilogue we watch the super-family at a stadium, cheering at Dash to slow down and pace up just sufficiently to be number two. When leaving the stadium they are met by the sight of a new monster ('the Underminer', ascending from underground on his giant screw) and happily put on their superhero masks, ready to fight the enemy once again.

In you more than yourself

In the figure of the superhero the animating principle becomes each hero's specific superpower, or, as Lacan would put it: 'that-which-is-in-you-more-than-yourself' (Lacan 1979: 263–76). As the superheroes go underground, this animating principle becomes something excessive, a surplus that has to be controlled. Again, the characters' problem seems to reflect the animators' problem. On the commentary track the director Brad Bird talks about the challenge of 'animating it without making it too big'. He does so as a commentary to the scene where Dash is in the car with his mother, after having been accused by his teacher for putting pins on his chair (which is true, but due to his incredible speed cannot be proved, even by video recordings played in slow motion). Bird explains how this scene was a difficult scene for the animators, the characters being in a closed space without speed and movement, the expressions on their faces being the central thing. 'Animating it without making it too big' is exactly the problem that Dash is having, having to control his special animating principle (running power) without completely giving it up, which is the equilibrium that he will reach at the end, guided by his family to be number two.

As with the whole problem of animation we here again seem to have a correspondence between the character's problem and Pixar's challenge. As noticed by J. P. Telotte (2010: 212), one could read Mr Incredible's opening remark as speaking also for Pixar: 'Who wants the pressure of being *super* all the time?' The pressure of being super is also the pressure of being Pixar. *The Incredibles* actually proves that Pixar has been able to cope with the pressure: in their first movie to feature human characters they impressively succeed in solving the technical difficulties in rendering human skin, texture, hair, clothing and wetness.

The problem of dealing with your animating principle as some kind of excess is strongly represented by the suburban part of the film: five people encaged in square houses, rooms, cars, offices, all of them having some special power which they are to repress. Especially, Mr Incredible suffers from this being

Figure 10 Mr Incredible encaged in his car. From *The Incredibles* (Brad Bird, 2004) © Pixar.

squeezed into too-tight spaces. As put by Telotte in his analysis of Pixar's space constructions: 'That conventionally three-dimensional world [...] simply does not fit his larger-than-life – and now fatter than most – physique' (Telotte 2010: 215).

One should notice how the superheroes' repressed special powers seem to be all congruent to the conventional nuclear family roles: the man's strength and need for action, the woman's hyper-flexibility, the boy's speed, the teenage girl's ability to protect herself through invisibility or creating a force field around herself, the baby who seems to contain the pure monstrous energy of the human child (which we know from Darla in *Finding Nemo* and Boo in *Monsters, Inc.*). Thus, they seem as just amplifications of something 'natural', whereas Syndrome's powers are artificial, prosthesis-like. Yet the repressed superpowers also deliver a critique of a nuclear family style in which the conventionally male value of physical strength and action is repressed, while the conventionally female virtue of flexibility is driven to its extremes, showing that it really takes a superwoman to be a housewife, as demonstrated in the hilarious dining scene when Elastigirl cannot help using her superpowers, stretching out her arms beyond any reality to keep the family table together.

Elastigirl is an heir to the elastic figures that the Russian film director Sergei Eisenstein celebrated in the 1940s when writing his notes and essays in praise of Disney. Linking Disney's elastic figures (like Mickey Mouse's arms stretching and growing to follow the tune of his singing) to other extraordinarily supple creatures from myths and circus, Eisenstein sees their 'plasmaticness', their 'transformability', as a utopian alternative to the 'standardization' and 'machine-like regularity' that he finds in American society (Eisenstein 2011: 15). As Ngai has pointed out, 'elasticity' in the post-Fordist era might as well mean supple subjection to power ('flexibility') as a liberatory potential to escape rigid forms (Ngai 2005: 100–1). Thus Mrs Incredible's superpower, her elasticity, could partly be seen as the flexibility it takes to adjust to the system, partly as carrying on that Utopian potential for metamorphosis that Eisenstein finds in early Disney.

As for Mr Incredible, the excess, the 'more-in-you-than yourself', seems at once to be the repressed superpower and the 'more-than-super' power that it takes to be a family man, as Elastigirl puts it at the moment of the wedding: 'You gotta be more than Mr Incredible, you know that, don't you?' (It is actually this question to which Mr Incredible answers: 'I do').

The film can be read as being about coming to terms with your 'superpower', understood as that monstrous excess that animates you, but must be controlled, as it is in the scene when Dash is guided to run at the right pace, not as fast as he can, but fast enough to be number two.

So, from one point of view the superpower is depicted as monstrous excess, which finds its purest expression in the baby Jack-Jack as he converts himself into fire at the end. This is a recurring Pixar point: the human child is a monster, and the task is to make the monstrous energy useful for society (cf. *Monsters, Inc.*). To Eisenstein, fire is the element of the animated cartoon, as it has the same capacity for metamorphosis, the same capacity to realize 'the dream of the flowing infinite diversity of the form' (Eisenstein 2011: 18). In his celebration of Disney, watching the images of a cartoon is like watching sun stains or a fire: 'They flicker, warm and cannot be caught' (Eisenstein 2011: 11). Thus Jack-Jack the fire baby could, just like Elastigirl's elasticity, also be seen as a leftover from the plasmatic transformability that Eisenstein finds in the early Disney cartoons, apart from being another figure of the infant as pure monstrous energy.

The 'super' not only functions as monstrous excess in the film, it also functions as imaginary identity and as signifier. One is tempted to regard the 'I' on the chest of Mr Incredible's suit ('I' for 'Incredible', the film's equivalent to 'S' for 'Superman') as a signifier that could mean 'imaginary', 'identity', and 'I'.

As for the question of identity, the film puts the question of whether the civil identity is the real identity of the superhero, or the super identity is the real identity of the civil person. When Frozone in the opening talk show scenes says that 'supergirls like to reveal their secret identity', 'secret identity' here means civil identity. But when Mr Incredible at the end unbuttons his shirt to reveal the 'I' on his suit, his secret identity is that of the superhero hiding beneath the civil person. This way the film deconstructs the idea of 'identity' as an innermost core; it rather becomes this evasive, moveable 'that-which-is-in-you-more-than-yourself'.

In Mr Incredible's pre-matrimonial life, 'super' means imaginary identity, the ideal ego. When his wife at the moment of the wedding asks him to be 'more-than-super', this 'super-super' marks the moment when imaginary identity is transgressed by the entering into the symbolic order, marriage as a symbolic castration through which Mr Incredible is subjected to his social position as husband and father. After this wedding/symbolic castration, 'super' comes to mean some kind of excess, some kind of excessive 'real' that animates the subject, but must be controlled. One might say that 'super' shifts between referring to the imaginary, the symbolic and the real dimension of the subject.

Jesus Christ superman

Eric Santner sees the animating principle of the subject as 'the surplus or excess of immanence' which is created when, through language and the big Other, we are inscribed into the symbolic order. At a moment he designates this 'surplus' by the prefix 'super' and the subject under its pressure as a 'superman'. This is the moment when he discusses Bataille's use of the prefix 'sur' (super/*über*). Santner remarks that in Georges Bataille's later work 'it is as if the prefix that formerly signified the posture of elevation, of standing above and over, has come to stand for the very surplus or excess of immanence that we have been tracking' (Santner 2011: 105). This could almost be a description of Mr Incredible's development, the prefix 'super' at the beginning signifying his being superior, but then becoming the excessive pressure from which he suffers when inscribed into the symbolic order as domesticated man.

Santner continues: 'The "superman" becomes, in this way, the one who has accepted responsibility for bearing a too-muchness, for being a placeholder of the flesh that exceeds any corporeal or corporate boundaries' (2011: 105). The human 'flesh' is something different from animal 'meat', it is what the meat becomes when inscribed into the symbolic order. Human flesh is always an incarnation, always incarnating a position within the symbolic order. Do we not get a glimpse of this suffering superman, the too-muchness of the flesh, when regarding Mr Incredible bending himself in the confinement of his much-too-small car? Is this image not related to the images Santner suggests to explain the too-much-ness being created by taking on the sociosymbolic sign? The king who has his excessive flesh created by the pressure of the crown, or the pope, as painted by Francis Bacon, whose face transforms into screaming, suffering flesh as he is dressed in his robe and confined to the cage of his throne. As a middle-class family man, Mr Incredible is neither a pope, nor a king, but as Santner explains, this is what happens in democracy: when there is no longer a sovereign, we all have to bear the burden of sovereignty, we all have to incarnate that 'super'. In democracy the sublime flesh of the sovereign is now a pressure under everyone's skin: 'every head now has a "body" of its own, one in which the symbolic, imaginary, and real elements of sovereignty push against the skin of its bearer' (Santner 2011: 140).

The super-image of incarnation in Christian culture, the image of Jesus Christ, is suggested when Mr Incredible hangs suspended ('crucified') in Incrediboy's torture machine, with an 'I' on his chest. Could we not read this as yet another image of the suffering from the excessive flesh that the superman takes on when subjected to/marked by the letter (the 'I')?

The image of superman in the torture machine actually blends the image of crucifixion with Leonardo da Vinci's famous 'Vitruvian Man', the man with the

Figure 11 Jesus Christ superman. From *The Incredibles* (Brad Bird, 2004) © Pixar.

geometrically ideal human proportions who has become famous as Manpower's logo. The two images are opposite ideals in our culture: the ultimate fragility of the flesh, crucified Christ, versus the quintessence of bodily human strength and perfection. Perhaps these are the two kinds of 'super' that Mr Incredible is suspended between: 'super' meaning on the one hand superman power, on the other hand the excessive and fragile flesh that the subject takes on through symbolic castration.

What Mr Incredible discovers while he is hanging there is finally his vulnerability, his weakness, his inability to bear the loss of his loved ones. As he has the opportunity to escape through sacrificing the life of Mirage (whom he for a moment takes as a hostage, while Syndrome does nothing to save her), Syndrome accuses him of weakness, but Mirage replies: 'valuing life is not weak'. This is a conventional way of conveying the Christian message, strength through weakness, but the way that the imagery indirectly depicts the two different kinds of 'super' seems to me more interesting.

Another mythical figure from Western culture is a clear reference in the film: the Greek titan Kronos. 'Kronos' is the name of Syndrome's mission to install himself as the new superman. In Greek mythology Kronos is the one who dethroned his father and ate his children, until he himself was dethroned by Zeus. This, of course, points to Oedipal rivalry between son and father, Incrediboy and Mr Incredible, as a basic theme of the film. From this perspective there is in the film a strife between the Greek myth in which father and son are struggling, and the Christian myth in which father and son become one in the image of crucified Christ. Kronos is the primal father (the one who has all the enjoyment), whereas Mr Incredible is the symbolically castrated father, whether he is encaged in his car or suspended like crucified Christ.

We are all individuals

To Syndrome, 'super' is some kind of phallus that he envies and wants to possess for himself. In his scornful speech to the super-family, as he freezes them and holds them suspended in the air, he mocks their 'precious gifts', their 'oh-so-special powers'. By his technological inventions (his artificial phallus) he wants to make it possible that 'everyone can be superheroes, everyone can be super', and concludes: 'When everyone is super, no one will be.'

Dash makes the same argument in the scene with his mother in the car: 'Everyone is special means that no one is special.' 'Everyone is special' could be said to be a persistent dogma in liberalist democracy, one of the most insistent and recurring messages in TV and films for children. Dash (and Syndrome) has realized that this dogma is a paradox. Actually it points to an immanent aporia in democracy: how is it possible to unite the principle of equality with the principle of the unique individual? An aporia which is expressed in lots of commercials for mass products appealing to the consumer's uniqueness: Don't be like anyone else, make your own choice, be very special – buy those Levi's jeans (like everybody else). Monty Python gets to the heart of this paradox in *Life of Brian*, in the scene where the crowd of people outside Brian's house uniformly shouts: 'WE ARE ALL INDIVIDUALS', except for one of them who raises a timid voice: 'I am not . . .'

The fantastic/the mundane

The film moves between two different worlds, the suburban universe of family life and the James Bondian universe of adventure. On the commentary track the two worlds are referred to as 'the mundane' and 'the fantastic', and the director Brad Bird explains how it is actually, in computer animation technique, much easier to make a fantastic world than a mundane one. One might say that computer animation technique is apt at rendering the imaginary (clear forms, smooth surfaces), but needs much work to be able to produce the flaws, imperfections and irregularities of reality. To animate the 'mundane' the 'super' needs to be transformed from imaginary identity to the excess of the flesh.

In his analysis of Pixar's animated space, Telotte also notices the shift between the 'mundane' (Telotte calls it 'domestic') and the 'fantastic' in *The Incredibles*. He shows how the everyday world is 'depicted in highly conventional cinematic techniques' (Telotte 2010: 214) activating the play between background and foreground through movements, parallel action and focal shifts. One might further notice how the colours in the mundane world, compared with the fantastic, are greyish and dim, kind of 'functionalist' colours in the style of the architecture and design of the 1950s.

Whereas the 'mundane' world is associated with a 1950s modernist style, the 'fantastic', according to Telotte, matches Hal Foster's characterization of postmodern architecture: 'a rhetorical front and conventional behind' (Telotte 2010: 209). The fantastic space of Syndrome's island is full of 'surprising facades, trick entries, and disguised passages': the entrance to the headquarters is behind a waterfall, the computer control room is behind a wall of lava (Telotte 2010: 215).

Just like I claim that the technical question of animation also becomes an important theme in the Pixar movies, so Telotte claims that the construction of space is both a technical and thematic issue: 'The space of narration [. . .] becomes the stuff of narration' (2010: 216). To Telotte, the film's central theme, the conflict between the everyday and the extraordinary, is to a great degree depicted in terms of space: the conventional space versus the space with depths that escape us.

I do not completely agree, though, that the 'mundane', suburban space in *The Incredibles* is a conventional three-dimensional realist space. The straight lines of the suburban streets and of the corridors at Mr Incredible's workplace, the squares of houses and offices, give us more the claustrophobic impression of being 'boxed'. Neither does the Nomanisan space suggest 'depths that escape us', rather does it suggest depth as something constructed, and its imaginary world is clearly shown as something limited, confined to the island.

We survived, but we are dead

When one transgresses the symbolic space, one might, in Lacanian terms, either move into the space of the imaginary or touch upon the real.

As we saw in the chapter on *Finding Nemo*, Lacan points to the tragic Greek heroine Antigone as a figure who has moved beyond the symbolic order into the zone of the real. She is, as Lacan puts it, 'between two deaths' (Lacan 1992: 270). As a citizen she is dead: King Creon has cast her out of society, because she defies his decree and insists on burying her dead brother, even if he has fought on the side of the enemy. Between Antigone's death as a citizen and her biological death ('between two deaths') is the zone where her acts have the necessity of the tragic hero, and she does what she has to do (bury her brother), even if it goes against the laws of society as well as the laws of self-sustainment.

The super-family's arrival on Nomanisan Island is accompanied by a line that actually marks an entrance into the zone between two deaths. When Elastigirl has saved her children to the shore, Dash exclaims: 'We're dead! We're dead! We survived, but we're dead!' Being dead, but yet not dead, cast out of their lives as citizens in suburban reality, the children seem to finally let themselves be animated by their inner drive (each by their special superpower) in a redemptive way. They may even be said to live after the commandment which is to Lacan the ethical commandment: 'Do not give up on your desire' (Lacan 1992: 319–21), that is, if we here understand each one's superpower as this kind of pure desire that makes the subject tick.

If the landing on Nomanisan Island seems to have the potential to open up a zone of the real (of the drive), it nevertheless ends up in the imaginary, the ideal image of the nuclear family that is so central to American ideology. As the family is on its way home, Dash exclaims: 'This is the best vacation I ever had, I love my family.'

The image of the nuclear family is fixated in two interestingly different ways in the Nomanisan part of the film. First, the four family members are encapsulated in the protective force field that Violet has the power to create. This is a kind of 'warm' fixation, created by the protective power from within the family itself. Then, the family is frozen by the point zero energy that Syndrome sends out from the finger of his glove. This is a cold fixation, created by a freezing energy from without the family. The ideal image of the warm and loving family is thus followed by what might be seen as its shadow side, the nuclear family as a fixed structure in which its members are frozen.

If we ask Judith Halberstam if *The Incredibles* has 'Pixarvolt', we will definitely get a negative answer. The film certainly has the two themes that according to Halberstam extinguish any potential Pixarvolt: 'family' and 'romance'. Actually, *The Incredibles* seems clearly to promote key features of American ideology: the nuclear family, vigilantism (represented by the superhero) and the liberalist-democratic dogma number one: 'Everyone is special.' Still, it might be said to have some 'volt' in its exposure of democracy's immanent aporia (how to combine equality and individualism?) and in its depiction of the excess of flesh (the 'super') which makes of the suburban family father a creature whose suffering is not unlike the suffering of Christ himself.

8

The Mother Road: *Cars*

Like the Disney classic *Herbie*, *Cars* fulfils the boyish dream of the living car. But what happens when driver and vehicle are collapsed into one image: the animated car? What is the fantasy of man and car becoming one all about?

Following Donald Crafton and Alan Cholodenko one might argue that the car as 'automobile' reflects the 'automobility' at stake in animation (Cholodenko 2007: 494–6). From a techno-historical perspective, Crafton sees the animated objects (furniture, tools, toys) of early animation as reflections of the 'wonderful inventions' of that time: the aeroplane and the automobile, 'moving with what seemed their own internal life' Crafton 1982: 1932). To induce the car with (human) autonomy might thus be only to take a step further its automobility, situating us once again in the zone of confusion between mechanization and animation. The motorized vehicle may seem endowed with a soul, and, as we shall see, a psychoanalyst may use the metaphor of 'motor' to describe the human 'drive', 'drive' being of course in itself a word connecting car and human.

Cars opposes the original 'mother road' moving with the land to the modern interstate 'cutting through' the land, touching upon ideas of the maternal body and the castrating father illuminated by psychoanalysis. From an ideological perspective on American history it is interesting how the film invests fantasies of origin and maternity into an early modernity, which is actually based on 'paternal' symbolic castration of nature. Despite the high valuation of the maternal I shall here argue that the decisive animating principle in the film becomes the desire to prevent paternal defeat, or to sustain paternal desire.

Cars (John Lasseter, Joe Ranft, 2006) is the story of Lightning McQueen (Owen Wilson), a young, super-talented racing car heading for 'the Piston Cup'. The opening scenes show him on the racing arena as a successful and overconfident 'rookie', dreaming of still more success. His signature is his catchphrase 'ka-chow!' as he poses in front of the camera and reflects the blitz as a lightning blink. As he is on the interstate in his truck (an animated car inside an animated truck), on his way to the final race for the Piston Cup, pushing his sleepy vehicle to keep driving in the night, he is cast off road and finds himself on Highway 66, appearing in the film like some dream-like 'other scene', leading him to the ghost-like town of Radiator Springs, a kind of David Lynchian fantasy of a 1950s town in which everything, including the traffic lights, is caught in meaningless, monotonous activity. Chased by a police car, he damages a road in the town and the next morning is sentenced to repair it, having to drag the old road-paving machine Bessie, which stains him with excremental asphalt.

The people of Radiator Springs form a typical population of off-road towns, including the hillbilly tow truck Mater (Larry the Cable Guy), the senile lady veteran car, the hippie VW van selling ecological fuel, the Italian tyre seller Luigi and his assistant Guido. Two of the town's inhabitants become leading characters in McQueen's story: the hot blue Porsche Sally (Bonnie Hunt), the town's attorney and motel owner who has left her stressed out life in LA behind, and the judge and doctor Doc Hudson (Paul Newman), a grumpy old Hudson Hornet whom McQueen discovers to have had a grand career as a Piston Cup winning race car until he was thrown out of the game by a crash. Sally becomes McQueen's love interest, and Doc his symbolic father.

At first feeling completely humiliated and trying to escape the 'hillbilly hell' for the Piston Cup race, McQueen slowly learns to appreciate the pace and values of the country town, doing his job well, scaring tractors (the cattle of the cars) with Mater, driving around without any goal in the beautiful landscape with Sally. Inspired by McQueen's new smooth black asphalt road the people give their town a make over and fix their neon to shine festively as the road is inaugurated by an evening of cruising. McQueen's relationship with his father figure, Doc Hudson, stays tense, though: the rookie does not want to learn from the veteran, and the bitter Doc does not want to confront his ruined past. As McQueen is discovered by the media (informed by Doc) and brought to the Piston Cup race, though, Doc takes (accepted by McQueen) the role of his coach.

Supported by Doc and his team from Radiator Springs, McQueen is just about to win the race, as one of his competitors, 'The King', is pushed off the lane by the other one, the disagreeable Chick Hicks, and crashes. Chick Hicks wins, as McQueen, remembering the old newspaper photo of Doc's crash, gives up his victory to get the crashed 'King' and push him over the finish line. The winner Chick Hick is booed, and the loser McQueen is celebrated and offered to be with his dream team Dinaco. But he rejects, choosing to have his team and headquarters in Radiator Springs. In the final scene we see McQueen and Sally happily cruising together in the beautiful landscape, and in the credits we see images of Radiator Springs re-blossoming, lots of cars choosing the exit from the interstate to take a detour through the town. Radiator Springs has been put 'back on the map'.

Movement and stasis

Cars is about speed and slowing down. It opposes the right line and the speed of the interstate to the curved line and the slowing down of Highway 66. And it opposes the large-scale space of the racing arena, with its mass public and fast flashing blinks, to the small-scale space of the town, with its character types and decorative neon.

As Telotte points out, movement is both a technical and thematic concern of the film. With this film Pixar introduced a new technique of motion blur, blurring objects to render the way we perceive them in motion (Telotte 2010: 217). This made it possible to blur the moving cars while keeping their facial details distinct (2010: 217–18), thus animating the cars in both of the word's senses: making them move and humanizing them. The technique as well as the story is about pace and movement, and Telotte stresses the connection between pace and space: it is due to McQueen's slowing down that Radiator Springs is put 'back on the map' (2010: 218), 'with that shift in speed, it seems, space itself has been rediscovered and reconfigured' (2010: 219).

If the blurring technique and the racing scenes make speed and movement a concern of the film, the central theme of the crash points to slowing down and stasis. In her brilliant book *Crash. Cinema and the Politics of Speed and Stasis*, Karen Beckman actually, by focusing on the theme of the crash, wants to shift the focus on cinema as the art of movement to cinema as the art of shifting between movement and stasis. She points to 'the critical paradigm' within film theory that 'aligns the automobile with the moving camera, the moving filmstrip, and the illusion of movement created in the act of projection' (Beckman 2010: 4), quoting Jean Baudrillard, Paul Virilio and Edward Dimendberg who all analogize the cinematic experience and the visual experience of car-driving. Baudrillard talks about the landscape 'unfolding like a televised screen' when one is driving a car; Virilio points to the images in the windshield as a kind of cinema; Dimendberg compares the visual experience of being on the highway to cinematic montage and multiplicity of perspectives (Beckman 2010: 4–5). In these ideas the car, as well as cinema, is associated with movement, but by focusing on the car crash Beckman herself rather wants to show the relationship between movement and stasis as central to cinematic art as well as to automobile culture (2010: 5).

Cars does not only oppose movement and stasis, it also opposes two different kinds of movement: the straight line and the curved. A recurring image is the image of the map, showing the curved line of Highway 66 running beneath the straight line of the interstate.

When the driver is a car

In Shakespeare's *Hamlet* (Act 4, scene 7) a reference appears to a French gallant by the allegorical name of 'Lamord'. As a man of non-hesitating action he serves as a counterpoint to Hamlet, and it is said of him (by Claudius) that 'he grew unto his seat/ and to such wondrous doing brought his horse/ as he had been incorpsed and demi-natured/ with the brave beast'. This fantasy of the resolute, energetic man as the man who has become one with his horse has a modern version in the fantasy of man and car becoming one. 'Incorpsed with the car' is exactly what has happened to Lightning McQueen who is car and driver in one.

Just like the horse in older literature, so the car in modern literature and film may serve as a metaphor for the character's drive, and the image of car and driver becoming one as a metaphor for man becoming one with his drive.

The drive is a central concept to psychoanalysis; it might actually be said to be *the* question central to psychoanalysis: what drives the subject? Relating the driving of the subject to car-driving, Karen Beckman adopts Jean Laplanche's definition of the drive as the subject's 'motor' which 'metabolises the enigmas that are put to [. . .] the subject from the outset by interhuman communication' (Beckman 2010: 20–1). Behind Laplanche's enigmas put to the subject by interhuman communication lurks Lacan's concept of 'the Other'. The Other exactly has this function of emanating enigmatic messages that the subject strives to interpret.

The audience forms an instance of 'the Other' to McQueen, emanating their blinks like enigmatic messages to which he responds by making the blink his own signature when posing in front of their gaze. The exchange of blinks makes of the relationship between subject (McQueen) and Other (audience) a flashy, shiny, imaginary one, which is also a mutual blinding. The story of McQueen is the story of having gradually to dis-identify with this shiny, flashy self-image, which happens clearly when McQueen is picked up from Radiator Springs by his truck, and there is discrepancy, no longer identity, between his bewildered appearance and his image on the truck's back door, behind which he is enclosed.

In the nightly ghost version of Radiator Springs that we meet at the beginning of the film, the drive has become pure, meaningless repetition: Luigi's assistant repeatedly correcting a tyre in the pile, the stoned hippie van stuck at watching the traffic lights blinking, claiming every third blink to be slower ('The sixties weren't good to you, were they?'). Through McQueen's arrival in the town, this drive is transformed into desire: a love story and a story of a town shining up to attract consumers. The town's energy is transformed from repetitive drive with no object *a*, to desire for love, consumers and success.

McQueen's will to victory originates in a completely black space. The screen is black when we are with McQueen behind his closed eyes as he prepares mentally for the competition ('I am a precision instrument of speed and aerodynamics'). Once he has been taken off-road and distracted by love interest, this black space of concentration is disturbed by images of amorous cruising through the landscape. A drive originating in some kind of void emptied of any images, a desire originating in the imaginary of the love story.

Beckman brings together the motive of the car with the theme of the 'stimulus shield' ('Reizschutz'), Freud's concept for a kind of psychic membrane protecting the subject from an excess of outer stimuli, which has become central to modernity theory through Walter Benjamin's prompting it as an important feature of urban man (Beckman 2010: 10). The car may seem as a materialization of modern man's protective shield, yet it is also a fragile shield, actually exposing man's body to lesions and death. Beckman draws towards an understanding of the stimulus shield as well as the car's metal and the cinematic screen as a porous interface between organism and world rather than a protective distance. A kind of skin, that is. By making car and driver one *Cars* seems to stress this connection, as the metal of the car literally becomes the characters' skin. What should be noticed, though, is the shiny plastic surface of the Pixar cars, notably McQueen, a kind of 'skin' that seems thick and smooth, almost invulnerable. The two crashed 'paternal' cars that appear in the film, Doc Hudson and 'The King', seem to have a more metallic and fragile surface, prone to be crumpled like a can.

The mother road, the father's body

In a wonderful metaphor Paul Virilio compares women to vehicles: 'Man is the passenger of woman', referring to man being inside woman, both in pregnancy and copulation. 'Woman is the first means of transportation for the species, the second one would be the horse', writes Virilio, and the modern one would be the car, still based on a woman's 'back' that is, according to Virilio, the 'infrastructure' from which 'all auto-mobility will stem'. At another point it is the highway, which seduces without really leading anywhere, that Virilio compares to (a prostituted) woman: 'It leads towards the horizon like the prostitute leading the soldier to her chamber' (quoted from Beckman 2010: 13).

In Marinetti's futuristic manifesto, the car is gendered as masculine, while the ditch into which it rolls is gendered as feminine: 'I spun my car around with the frenzy of a dog trying to bite its tail [. . .] I stopped short and to my disgust rolled over into a ditch with my wheels in the air . . . O maternal ditch, almost full of muddy water! Fair factory drain! I gulped down your nourishing sludge; and I remembered the blessed black breast of my Sudanese nurse . . .' (Beckman 2010: 18). Notice how car and man become one (in the metaphor of the dog biting its own tail, and the first person possessive pronoun: 'my wheels'), forming one masculine unit plunging into, and pleasurably engulfing, the maternal muddy water.

In *Cars* the highway is not a prostitute, but Route 66 is definitely maternal, 'the mother road'. The paving road machine that stains McQueen with excremental black asphalt is explicitly feminine, Bessie, thus partly joining Marinetti's maternal muddy ditch and Sudanese nurse.

When Sally tells McQueen of the time before the highway, flashback images and the nostalgic song 'Long ago, but no so long ago' illustrate and accompany her story. Sally explains the difference between Route 66 and the highway thus: 'It didn't cut through the land, it moved with the land. It rose, it fell, it curved.' The two different types of road are associated with two different kinds of time, the quantitative and the qualitative: 'Cars didn't drive on it [Route 66] to make great time, but to have a great time.' The highway's 'cutting through' the land has something of the paternal symbolic castration about it, while the 'moving with' is associated with the 'mother road'. The 'moving with' refers to woman as 'the first means of transportation for the species' (cf. Virilio), the maternal body with which the foetus and the infant move. The difference between the 'cutting through' and the 'moving with' the landscape is clearly illustrated by the image of the map, in which the straight, thick line of Highway 40 is drawn beneath the thin, curved line of Route 66.

Route 66 is in the film imbued with connotations of nature (organic lines and movement, associated with the maternal), whereas the highway is cultural violence against that nature, associated with the paternal. But this is of course a kind of retroactive projection of something 'natural' into just an earlier cultural construction. Route 66 and the cars of earlier generations were just as much a technological intervention into nature as the highway. One even shudders a little when 'fixing the neon' is the culmination of the restoration of this earlier and more 'natural' world. From an ecological perspective the neon has surely lost its innocence. The ecological perspective that is missing in *Cars* (2006) is taken up in the sequel, *Cars 2* (2011). Here the plot evolves around fake alternative fuel, and Lightning McQueen actually has his life saved by the hippie van's 'all-natural, sustainable organic biofuel'.

In *Cars*, slowing down is associated with a return to the maternal. Sally's motel 'The Cosy Cone' is also an image of this. The cone's phallic form is usually a sign of hindrance, but Sally's cones are opening like wombs to receive the guests.

Cars seems to be critical to juvenile speed and paternal 'cutting through' in favour of maternal staying or 'moving with'. But in the plot the desire to prevent paternal defeat becomes decisive. The image of the crashed car functions as an image of the defeated father. In a strangely obscene scene, right before McQueen sneaks into Doc's garage to discover his Piston Cups, he looks at his 'medical' consultation (that is, car repair shop), slightly shocked to see the sheriff (a 1949 Mercury Police Cruiser) hanging from the roof, having some kind of treatment of his bottom. The sheriff's bottom is clearly showing, a jack plugged into it like some kind of anal penetration. The sexual connotation, putting McQueen in the role of the voyeur, is underlined by Doc's words as McQueen leaves: 'I hope you enjoyed the show!' This is some kind of primal scene, Doc in the role of the penetrating (father), the sheriff in the role of the penetrated (father). The scared expression on McQueen's face makes of him the child in the primal scene, shocked to discover the sexual activities of his parents.

The display of the paternal figure's private parts has a reverberation in *Cars 2*, in which the leader of the villains appears, transmitted on screens, as just an open hood revealing the parts of his motor. As if we get to look into his guts. The villain of *Cars 2* is apparently a producer of alternative fuel, but secretly the leader of the 'lemon' cars who want to gain power and influence by making the world dependent on their large untapped oil reserve. In *Cars 2* he is all by himself split into two figures: the fake role of the caring, benevolent father who wants to save the world, and his identity as a villain; but his putting his guts on display echoes Doc's bottom on display in *Cars*, making of him a kind of perverted echo of the symbolic father.

McQueen's primal scene is the relationship between the father in control and the defeated father, a theme which is repeated in the following as McQueen at first discovers the signs of Doc's former victories, the Piston Cups in the garage, and later the sign of his defeat, the newspaper image on the wall showing Doc's crash. The Piston Cups are devaluated as soon as they are discovered: Doc calls them 'just empty cups', and as McQueen shouts out his discovery to the town's people 'He won the Piston Cup', Mater asks 'He did what on his cup?' Mater's line reveals the homophony between 'Piston Cup' and 'pissed on cup', somehow continuing the vulgar tone from the repair scene and through the pun condensing victory and defeat in one.

In his juvenile hubris McQueen's aim has been to defeat the father, but from this point in the film (the repair and garage scenes) he is still more animated by the wish to restore the defeated father, culminating in the final race when he sacrifices his own victory in order to get the crashed 'King' over the finish line. The son sacrificing himself to glorify the father, thereby actually winning a victory much more glorious than the ruthless, competitive winner – this theme is not without Christological connotations.

Through the trope of the animated car the film is about the relationships between man and drive, between movement and stasis, speeding up and slowing down, 'moving with' and 'cutting through', the maternal and the paternal. It points to the 1950s as a historical landscape which has taken in the American imagination the position of some kind of natural origin, even if it is just an earlier state of technological modernity. And despite its celebration of a maternal 'moving with', the drive that animates the plot in the end is the son's wish to prevent or make up for the humiliation of the father.

Pixar celebrates the idiot and itself: *Cars 2*

The sequel, *Cars 2* (John Lasseter, Brad Lewis, 2011), is a James Bond pastiche focusing on the character of Mater who is mistaken for a spy and becomes involved with the British intelligence service as he is in Japan with Lightning

McQueen for a world race organized by the apparent inventor of the alternative fuel 'allinol', Sir Miles Axlerod, who turns out to be a villain. Mater's story is the story of the simple and unmannered country hick who is let down by his embarrassed friend (as McQueen feels ashamed of him in the high society of racing cars), but finally becomes the hero, the one who saves McQueen's life. But how can a country hick become an efficient secret agent? The film gives two answers: through his low-tech competence (whereas the British agents are top tuned in digital technology, Mater is able to identify any old motor or bolt, which finally makes him identify the villain), and through his surroundings' misinterpretation of his simplicity. For a long time the British agents, mistaking Mater for another agent, think that he plays the idiot, not that he is one. But Mater is a true example of Groucho Marx's line: 'This man looks like an idiot and acts like an idiot, but this should in no way deceive you, he IS an idiot' (quoted by Slavoj Žižek 1991: 73). So his idiocy is interpreted as 'idiocy', and he is saved by the secret service computer system as it misinterprets what he is saying: when he says 'dad gum' (his euphemism for god damned) it provides him with 'gatling guns'; when he says 'I didn't mean that kind of shoot', it provides him with a 'chute'.

The Groucho Marx line is quoted by Žižek to illustrate the Lacanian dictum: 'Those who do not let themselves be duped, are mistaking' (in French, *les non-dupes errent*, punning on *les noms du père*, 'the names of the father'). Lacan's point is that to enter into the symbolic order (to which you are initiated by 'the name of the father', the name that inscribes you into social and linguistic order) also means to enter into a world of signs that you should know when not to take by their face value. Metaphor, the operation of transferring meaning, is the prototypic operation of the symbolic order. Not to understand metaphor (not to let yourself be duped) is to not be integrated into the symbolic order. To make of the idiot a hero, *Cars 2* has to make face value conquer symbolic value. This happens when Mater, towards the end, has a bomb placed inside his motor and warns Lightning McQueen on the racetrack, 'I am the bomb', which is metaphorically interpreted by McQueen as, 'Yes, you are the bomb.' Face value is the truth, metaphor is on the villains' side. This is also the case when Mater's warning 'you will be killed' is drowned by the villain tow truck Ivan who transforms 'kill' into metaphor: 'You killed out there' (referring to McQueen's performance in the race).

The gang of villains in *Cars 2* introduce another answer to the question: what animates the subject? – 'The inner lemon' . . . The villains are old-fashioned cars, 'lemons'. They are driven by their desire for recognition, their resentment about being regarded as outdated and ridiculous. Their motto is 'Embrace your inner lemon, let it drive you'. The gang is based in Europe, its leader is British (voiced by Eddie Izzard), and the scientific leader Professor Zündap (voiced by Thomas Kretschmann) has a strong German accent and wears a Nazi monocle. 'The inner lemon' is actually not an unprecise diagnosis of what is driving many subjects in populist Europe these days: resentment.

John Lasseter has pronounced that he had the idea for *Cars 2* while overseas on a promotional tour for the first *Cars*, having fun imagining his animated cars in the different countries that he visited. Thus, in *Cars 2*, we go to Tokyo, to London, to Paris, to the Italian Riviera, so many occasions for the animators to customize their cars in different national styles: the geisha car, the Italian Big Mama car, the two Citroëns kissing on the Parisian bridge, and so on. This costumizing becomes a meta-theme when Mater is provided with a computerized disguising program, so that he can change in a split second from American hillbilly truck to Tyrolean in 'materhosen' to Transylvanian vampire. This kind of instant and complete makeover is what computer technology can do, thus the film once again seems not least to be a celebration of its own technology. The journey from place to place on the world atlas that accompanies the credits ends in the Bay Area, showing a gigantic Pixar Luxor lamp as its hallmark. Pixar celebrates itself.

9

Man is a Puppet, Soul is a Rat: *Ratatouille*

Ratatouille is the Pixar film that seems to have the most imaginative answer to the question: What animates the human being? – A small rat hidden under the hat. *Ratatouille* gives us the strangely touching, completely weird image of the most anonymous kitchen boy Linguini being directed to cook fabulous dishes by the rat Remy who is sitting on his head, pulling his hair like the strings of a marionette, hidden by his traditional white toque. The marionette as a metaphor for the human being is not new in the Western history of thought, but the rat as a metaphor for the human *animus* or soul certainly is.

In the chapter on *The Incredibles* I found Lacan's concept of the 'in-you-more-than-yourself' to be exemplified by the special power of the superheroes. In the following I shall focus on the ambivalent character of the 'in-you-more-than-yourself', excremental and sublime, that I find to be united in the figure of the master chef rat. The rat will further be understood as a figure that transfers unto the leading male character his father's desire. Finally I want to examine how the film deals with the theme of 'love', partly as something induced by the Parisian setting, partly as the true love story between the rat and the culinary critic, illustrating Lacan's dictum: 'Love is giving something one does not have to someone who does not want it.'

Anyone can cook

Ratatouille (Brad Bird, Jan Pinkava, 2007) is told, by means of voice-over, from the retrospective perspective of the rat Remy (Patton Oswalt) himself. The introduction to the film shows a television set freely flowing in the universe, pointing to the illuminating function of salvation that TV will actually have in the film. Then Remy introduces himself by a frozen cliffhanger: we see him breaking his way through the windowpanes of a country house, having his image frozen as he is suspended in the air, clinging to a book of recipes and a spatula.

His story is then told, first in flashback up to the point of the breaking through the windowpane, then from that point onwards.

Living with his big rat family in the French countryside on the ceiling of an old lady's house, Remy has an odd passion for fine cooking. From the leftovers of food to be found among the garbage he selects fine pieces and combines them into exciting sensations of taste that he tries to share with his fellow rats, and he is completely spellbound when the face of the Parisian chef Gusteau (Brad Garrett) appears on the old lady's TV, claiming that 'everyone can cook'. Among the rats, though, his talent is used for the simple purpose of survival: his father makes him sniff at garbage items to check if they are edible.

One day he and a friend are discovered in the kitchen by the old lady who gets her gun and shoots at Remy suspended in a lamp hanging from the ceiling. She misses Remy, but the ceiling cracks and reveals the huge population of rats, taking flight as the lady, dressed in a gas mask like a soldier from the First World War, continues her shooting. This is the point when Remy breaks through the window.

The dramatic scene of shooting and revelation plays with the change of perspective: for some moments we experience the situation from the perception of the old lady, the articulated words of the rats turning into squeaking, and when the ceiling falls down we do also for a moment adopt a 'human' perspective, feeling the unpleasant creepiness of this mass of disgusting animals, and the shock of this 'other world' breaking through the border (clearly marked by the ceiling) of the human one.

Lost behind the rest of the rats, Remy undertakes his lonely travel through the underworld, sailing in the gutters, using the recipe book as his boat, and the spatula as his oar, until, helped by the fantasy image of the chef Gusteau, he finally pops up in Paris, in the deceased Gusteau's old restaurant.

The restaurant has been taken over by the greedy, choleric and tiny Mr Skinner (Ian Holm), and the day when Remy arrives also brings the arrival of a young Mr Nobody by the name of Alfredo Linguini (Lou Romano) asking for a job. Being employed as a 'garbage boy' one of Linguini's first tasks is to throw out Remy, caught in a cage, in the Seine, but through his identification with the rat, and his discovering of its ability to communicate, he brings it home instead. Here begins the bond between man and rat that leads to the installation of a rat under a man's hat, directing him to cook fabulous dishes that amaze the customers at the restaurant, and make Linguini advance from garbage boy to cook. Linguini is taught by the tough and only woman in the kitchen, Colette

(Janeane Garofalo) – a relationship starting in jealousy, but ending in love (generating Remy's jealousy).

The kitchen chef turns out to be a real villain, not only misusing Gusteau's name as a brand for fast food products, but also hiding the letter that reaches him from Linguini's dead mother, telling that Linguini is actually – Gusteau's son … It is Remy the rat who gets to read this letter and, after having been chased through Paris by the kitchen chef, makes Linguini read it and take his righteous place as the owner of the restaurant.

Remy himself is having trouble with his base, the rat world, as he meets them again, and they want him to steal food from the kitchen for them, while his father is trying to talk him out of mixing with the human world, showing him as a warning the dead bodies of trapped and poisoned rats in the window of a shop for pest control. As Linguini discovers Remy having given his family access to the pantry, he throws him out.

In the decisive scene towards the end the most famous restaurant critic in Paris, the vampire-like Anton Ego (Peter O'Toole), arrives at Gusteau's, waiting for his food to be served, while a drama is enacted in the kitchen: due to their controversy, Remy has left Linguini, but returns – Linguini reveals his secret and introduces his 'little chef' to the staff, who take their leave, leaving Linguini, Colette and Remy alone in the kitchen. Remy calls for his fellow rats and organizes them as an army of cooks, producing the simple dish that he wants to serve to the great critic: *Ratatouille.*

The scene when Anton Ego puts the fork to his mouth, tasting the ratatouille, is magical, on a high with the scene in Proust when the narrator dips his *madeleine* in tea and by the taste of it is mentally transferred to the idyllic landscape of his childhood. The same thing happens to Anton Ego: suddenly he disappears into a tunnel of remembrance – we see him as a small, crying boy, having hurt himself, entering into his mother's kitchen, being comforted by the dish she puts before him: ratatouille … Completely satisfied, Ego wants to see the chef, and the sight of Remy the rat makes him write in his enthusiastic review that now he finally understands Gusteau's motto, everyone can cook, meaning not that we all have a talent for cooking, but that talent can be found in the most unexpected places. With this review Gusteau's restaurant has reached its complete triumph – while being closed down by the pest control. In the end, though, Colette and Linguini have opened another, less pretentious 'bistro' by the name of 'Ratatouille' and here we find, on the ceiling, Remy telling his story to his fellow rats enjoying their meal at rustic tables, and in the full, packed bistro

Anton Ego, dressed in a beret as a man of the people, ready to enjoy what Remy may cook for him: 'Surprise me!'

French accent

The film is provided with a certain charming 'Frenchness'. The voices of (most of) the human characters have a French accent, thus almost making this a mark of humanity – whereas the rats, clearly the 'negroes' of this film, playing jazz and being persecuted, speak with an American accent. The only human character with an American accent is Linguini, thus marked as somehow related to the rats. 'Frenchness' gets to connote aesthetic refinement, distinguishing human from animal. Proust is in the air, not only in the deeply touching scene when Anton Ego has his experience of *mémoire involontaire*, opening him to a hyper-sensuality where he can clearly hear the sound of a pen falling on the carpet, but also in the artistically interesting ambition to visualize smell and taste, that is to proceed by that cross-over of the senses called in ancient Greek stylistics 'syn-aesthesis' (co-sensing). Whereas Proust worked to make writing represent subtle impressions of all the senses, Pixar here works to make images and sounds represent smell and taste, in the scene showing Remy's brother taste the combination of burnt mushroom, pecorino cheese and rosemary, figuring him isolated on a black background, while the different sensations of taste are represented by abstract, coloured, moving, combining figures above his head, accompanied by notes that also combine into melody and harmony – until he has no more concentration, and the show of colours and music suddenly, with a comical effect, stops.

The 'Frenchness' of the film also resides in its insisting, like so many Hollywood films, on Paris as the site of love. The love story of Linguini and Colette is preceded and accompanied (and as I shall later claim: almost incited) by a series of background images of man and woman in love in Paris. One of these images appears when Remy pops up in Paris and through a window in the roof watches a scene between two lovers in an apartment: the woman seemingly about to stab the man with a knife, but the murderous gesture turning into a loving embrace. This may even be to honour the affinity between love and murder celebrated by Francois Truffaut: to film love like murder, and murder like love (Truffaut 1986: 345). French film is also honoured in the surname of Colette: Mademoiselle Tautou, referring to French actress Audrey Tautou who became famous for her performance in *Le fabuleux destin d'Amélie Poulain* (2001).

The rat as factor X

'I am not your puppet, you are not my puppet control guy', thus Linguini to Remy in an angry moment, thereby, by the figure of negation, confirming that this is exactly what they are. The idea of the human being as a marionette is known from the German romantic writer Heinrich von Kleist's famous essay 'Über das Marionettentheater' (1810), in which he brings together the most unconscious and the most conscious forms of life (*Gliedermann* and *Gott*, 'puppet' and 'God') as both expressions of the divine. With Kleist, the complete lack of reflectivity meets with hyper-reflectivity as two ways to reach the absolute. The human body having made itself a puppet is filled with that divine consciousness in which reflectivity culminates. The character of Linguini could be seen as a late heir to this romantic idea, but also exposing its comic potential, and replacing the abstract concept of divine consciousness with the image of a rat.

The puppet as unconscious body is in *Ratatouille* performed with great comic effect in the scene where Linguini has fallen asleep on duty, drunk from the wine his boss has poured into him, and Colette finds him in the morning. Remy is on place and actually manages to control the sleeping body, its closed eyes hidden by sunglasses, so that it looks awake, even if its expressions and sounds look to Colette like insults.

Whereas in Kleist something divine is controlling the human body, one might wonder what is controlling Linguini's body – what is the rat? What kind of image does one get for the soul from making it a rat?

The figure of the gourmet rat seems to concentrate two different aspects of the theme of 'excess': the disgusting and the sublime, as if establishing or stressing some kind of affinity between the superfluous as luxury and as garbage. Taking one of the most disgusting animals to human beings, the rat, and turning it into a representative of something utterly delicious, is one of the film's basic and interesting gestures. In this context the scene of the breaking ceiling in the first part of the film becomes important, as it actually for a moment gives us the rats from the human perspective – squeaking, disgusting and far too many.

In the last lecture of seminar XI (Lacan 1979: 293–307) Lacan speaks of *ce qui est en toi plus que toi* – 'that which is in you more than yourself' – as that at which love is directed. What we love in another person is this indefinable *je-ne-sais-quoi*, this 'in-you-more-than-you', this immanent excess. In show business it is called the 'X factor', and it seems to have this very ambiguous status between sublimity and shit.

In the Danish version of *American Idol* there once appeared a very young boy with a very big voice, singing almost like an adult tenor even though he was just a small kid. The impression was scary, confirming Žižek's definition of the voice as the alien inhabiting our bodies (Žižek in Fiennes 2006, *The Pervert's Guide to Cinema*). When the judges repeatedly exclaimed: 'It is unbelievable that such a big voice can be inside such a small boy', my twelve-year-old son, watching the show with me, made an immediate and thoroughly Lacanian commentary, quoting a line from a children's book I had once read to him: 'It is unbelievable that such a big shit can be inside such a small dog.' This commentary completely captured what I am getting at: the ambiguity of this immanent excess, excremental or sublime. In *Ratatouille* the rat, traditionally an excremental creature, is connected as well to the sublime – or its dealing with excess in the form of garbage is replaced by its dealing with excess in the form of fine cuisine. And hiding in Linguini's toque it could surely be said to be 'that which is in him more than himself'.

The rat in the toque might in a broader sense be seen as an allegory of the 'more' inhabiting human beings. This 'more' than mere survival, more than self-sustainment, more than pure need. This 'more' that has made an art out of cooking. If food were only about need and survival, French cuisine would not exist. As the culinary critic Anton Ego puts it: 'I do not like food, I love food.' 'Liking' is for the needing, not for the 'loving', being driven by their desire for this 'extra', this surplus of sensation that makes of eating an aesthetic experience. In the voices of the film this 'more' could be said to be the French accent, conventionally a sign of high culture, being here reserved for the human characters (except Linguini). Having a French accent in the film means having this 'extra'. 'Frenchness' is the very *je-ne-sais-quoi* marking the human characters and desired by the film-makers.

There is one accent that is a stigma in the film rather than a sign of noblesse, and that is the Indian accent of the kitchen chef's companion in selling fast food. By projection, fast food and commercialism, being truly American phenomena, are represented as something Indian.

That which is in Anton Ego more than himself, is called 'appetite' when Linguini gets it all wrong in his anxious exclamation: 'Appetite is coming, and he is bringing his Ego.' Getting it all wrong is of course getting it all right, in this truly Freudian slip revealing the 'ego' to be an object (or puppet) manipulated by the 'more' of the desire. One might discuss whether Ego's 'appetite' should be more precisely understood as 'drive' rather than 'desire', as it stubbornly circulates around the sublime culinary Thing rather than jumps from one object to another.

The rat seems to be a perfect allegory of the 'factor' that, according to Žižek, 'dispossesses the subject, reducing him to a puppet-like level' (Žižek 2006: 48). This 'more' inhabits the subject and sometimes makes him dance spasmodically, as does Linguini in the beginning when the rat has just moved into his toque. Linguini's relationship to the rat could be read as his gradually learning to live with this 'more' inhabiting him – developing from something that bites and stigmatizes him into something controlling him mildly and harmoniously like the dancer leads his lady.

Cooking, reading, TV watching

The 'more' inhabiting the human body is what makes it something different from an animal. Or, to quote Žižek from Sophie Fiennes' *Pervert's Guide*: 'Humanity means: the alien is controlling our animal bodies.' What distinguishes human from animal is an explicit theme in the film, being put into words by Remy who is the one aspiring to move from animal to human. 'Humans do not just survive', Remy says, thereby marking 'survival' as that which drives the animal, whereas something-more-than-survival (psychoanalysis would say: something even more forceful than the instinct to survive) drives human beings. In one scene Remy's desire for the sublime taste very literally shows itself stronger than his instinct to survive: this is when he climbs with his brother onto the roof of the country house in order to smoke a stick with mushroom and *tomme-de-savoie* over the chimney. Accidentally the stick is struck by lightning, throwing the rats off the roof and almost killing them, but giving to the cheese and mushroom a wonderful taste that makes Remy completely happy, wanting to do it all over again.

The rat community puts Remy's extraordinary senses to serve survival, using them to distinguish between poisonous and edible food, whereas to Remy himself they open up the field of aesthetics as more-than-survival. The distinction between animal and human could also be put in terms of the distinction between need and desire that Lacan takes over from Hegel. Need is common to animal and human and can be fulfilled, whereas desire is the human mark of distinction and can never (or only provisionally) be fulfilled. The art of fine cooking brings food from the realm of need into the realm of desire: the gourmet still looking for new inventions and sensations to surprise his palate, thus the claim of Anton Ego at the end of the film, 'Surprise me!' And thus the customers in the restaurant get bored after a while with Remy's fabulous soup that has given back Gusteau's its reputation, asking for 'something else'.

In the first part of the film, Remy, speaking to his brother, defines the distinctive traits of humanity as 'cooking, reading, TV watching'. As we have seen, 'cooking' is what turns food from an object of need into an object of desire (an *objet petit a*). 'Reading' marks the human subject as a linguistic being, a *parlêtre*, as Lacan calls it, this being itself a signifier, being named by the desire of its parents, having its place in the world assigned by the laws of language. Finally, 'TV watching' may seem a mark of humanity in its modern stupidity or consuming passivity, but when related to the role that TV plays as a theme in *Ratatouille* (and in other Pixar films), it rather marks the Other as that which animates the human being, that which installs desire at the core of the human subject. It is actually by watching TV that Remy comes to know his desire (to cook). In the figure of Gusteau, Remy's big Other emanates from the TV screen, telling him what he actually wants and how to get it, affirming Lacan's dictum that the desire is always the desire of the Other. Thus Remy and Lacan seem to agree on the traits defining humanity, whether called 'cooking, reading, TV watching' or 'desire, language, and the Other'.

The rat is the Negro of the world

As shown, Rémy himself, placed in Linguini's toque, becomes an allegory of that 'more' animating the human subject – clearly not symbolizing the animal, but rather the animus, in the human being.

The figure of the rat also has other allegorical functions in the film. At moments, and with a rather comical effect, it is staged as a potential penis: before finding a hiding place for the rat in his toque, Linguini for a moment considers hiding it in the front of his trousers, and the phallic allusion in Colette's remark, 'he calls it his little chef', when asked by the press about Linguini's source of inspiration, can hardly pass unnoticed by the adult part of the public. As a phallus the rat may be seen as yet another allegory of desire; as a penis it is rather a partial object having its own independent life which makes it rather an instance of 'the real'.

Another allegorical function of the rat relates to the theme of artistic creation. The rat world is staged as a kind of underworld to the human one, and the film seems to say that some contact with the underworld is needed in order to be an artist. Thus, as Colette explains it to Linguini, the cooks creating sublime food in Gusteau's kitchen are smugglers, compulsive gamblers and other kinds of criminals. This makes the kitchen a kind of underworld (or backstage) to the restaurant, just as the rat world is an underworld to the human one.

The rat of course also enters into that big theme of 'the other' that one can be sure to find in every American product of popular culture today. The rat becomes a metaphor of the social or ethnic 'other' as the worker, the Afro-American, the Jew. Compared with the universe of fine cooking, the rat world of hard work and pure survival may be seen to represent the working class, just as the loft of the rats compared with the restaurant is a kind of cozy but simple pub. In this context the American accent of the rats connotes a lower social class than the French accent of the human beings, whereas the Indian accent of Skinner's fast food companion is a stigma rather than a sign of noblesse. The allusion to African American culture is evident when the rats are playing jazz. Finally, the rats are staged as Jews when the old lady is trying to gas them, and when their dead bodies are shown on display in the window of the pest control, as victims of mass killing.

Then again, what is the effect of staging 'the other' (ethnic or social) as a rat? On the one hand it may seem a harsh concretization of the rat as a conventional racist metaphor for the other, used for the Jews by Nazis as well as Arabs. On the other hand, it might be seen as an appropriate metaphor for the 'neighbour' as defined by Slavoj Žižek: the abject one that I should love, the monstrous thing at

Figure 12 The rats as victims. From *Ratatouille* (Brad Bird, 2007) © Pixar.

my side – the parasite (Žižek 2005: 42–4). Žižek's point about 'the other' as my neighbour, leaning on Eric Santner and Giorgio Agamben, is that he is defined not by his 'humanity' but by his non-humanity. What I should love in the other, in order for him to become my 'neighbour' in the Judaeo-Christian sense, is that which is the most difficult to embrace, in another human being as well as in myself: that non-humanity at our core, being incarnated by figures such as the 'Muselmänner' in the concentration camps. The neighbour, as Žižek defines him, is an abject figure, a piece of garbage, just like the rat.

Thus *Ratatouille* may be said to take seriously the conventional racist metaphor for the other as a rat, instead of dismissing it as politically incorrect: yes, the other is a rat, and therefore you should love him. Or: love thy neighbour as a rat. One might object, of course, that the rats in the film are humanized to a degree that removes anything rat-like or abject about them, but actually the scene in the country house when we, for a few moments, experience the rats from a human perspective, squeaking and rushing down from the falling ceiling in lots, succeeds briefly in making us feel them as something disgusting, turning the ceiling into that border to the 'real' which cannot break down without a horrifying effect.

Still, I think the force and originality of the figure of the rat is more in its being a figure of the animating principle than its being a figure of the other.

Fathers and sons

So, *Ratatouille* gives us a picture of the soul as coming from the abject world, and the human body being just its marionette. At the same time, by humanizing the abject soul, the film could be said not to answer, but just to defer or redouble the question of what animates us, because if the soul itself has desires (if it 'cooks, reads, and watches TV'), it must itself have some kind of soul, some kind of 'puppet control guy', Remy's control guy being his symbolic father Gusteau.

The theme of sons and fathers, which is a recurrent theme in Pixar, is also very present in *Ratatouille*. Remy's staying true to his desire implies his replacing his biological father with Gusteau as a symbolic father figure. Linguini's story is very much a story about the entering of the name-of-the-father in his life (as it is revealed that he is actually Gusteau's son) that turns him from Mr Nobody into Mr Someone. It is almost as if the rat can transfer unto Linguini his father's desire, thus being some kind of libidinous support or preparation for his receiving the name-of-the-father as something purely formal. In this way Remy the rat is even a figure for that truth about desire that Lacan states in seminar XI: Desire is the father's desire (Lacan 1979: 38). Both Remy and Linguini have their origin in Gusteau's desire, but whereas Linguini is just its biological product, not really being animated by anything until Remy arrives, Remy takes on or even incarnates this desire.

Whereas Remy lets himself be guided by the voice of the big Other emanating from the TV, Linguini seems completely caught in the gaze of the big Other, the limelight of the media – the image of his horrified face in the flashlight of the photographers from the newspapers is a perfect illustration of the subject caught in the gaze of the big Other as a hare in the cone of light from a car (and a counterpoint to Woody in *Toy Story 2* being caught by the same kind of gaze, but completely seduced by it rather than scared).

Ah, l'amour . . .

Ratatouille is also a love story, the story of love between Linguini and Colette. But what kind of love story is it? Does the relationship between Linguini and Colette deserve the name of love? What kind of couple are they? Are they man and woman? Or do they seem to be Mr Nobody and Miss One-of-the-Boys, that is, rather sexless?

One interesting thing in the story of their relationship is Colette's line in a moment of disappointment with Linguini: 'I thought you were different', because if there is something Linguini is NOT, it is 'different' – he really has this character of Mr Nobody which makes him the perfect puppet. But of course, in a world where everyone is special (the other guys in the kitchen all have obscure and adventurous, more or less criminal, pasts), Mr Nobody can become the one who is different.

In their relationship, Remy the rat plays the function of the phallus. Linguini is the one who has got the phallus (the rat) just by chance, whereas Colette, as she sees herself, has been working twice as hard as the men to get her 'phallus', that is her position, her recognition as a cook.

Linguini's love and Remy become kind of rivals: Remy wants Linguini to cook and not to kiss, but actually the force of love in Linguini's arms is stronger than the force of Remy his control guy.

Actually the theme of love enters the film as a kind of French or Parisian topos rather than as an affect in the characters. The love scene as a theme appears at first on the TV in the old lady's house and then when Remy, on his flight from the house, arrives in Paris and looks into an apartment where a murder scene between man and woman turns into a kissing scene. (This Truffaut-like blend of murder and embrace could actually be seen as the primal scene not only of human existence, but also of the art of film: what is happening between man and woman in film, and in the small child's vision, imagined or real, of his parents' coitus, is love and murder in an indistinguishable blend.) The image of man and woman kissing or flirting reappears several times in the outdoor scenes of the film as this emblem of Paris which seems to belong necessarily to the *quais* of the Seine. One can get the feeling that the theme of love is induced by the Parisian setting rather than by some narrative logic.

If there is some truth to the Lacanian dictum that 'Love is giving something one does not have to someone who does not want it', we could see love as happening between Linguini and Colette as Linguini gives the talent (for cooking) that he does not have to Colette who certainly does not want it, being in a feminist rage with this young man showing up from nowhere and taking the place in the kitchen that she has worked so hard (twice as hard as the men, she says) to get.

The rat could clearly be said to be 'something in Linguini more than himself' which is Lacan's definition of the object of love at the end of seminar XI. But then again, is it the rat that Colette loves? Colette actually does not seem to go for that in Linguini which is in him more than himself – what she loves is rather the empty sack: Linguini as he walks into the kitchen being Mr Nobody and yet (or thereby) appearing to her as 'different'.

If 'love' in the Lacanian sense happens in *Ratatouille*, it is perhaps rather in that which stays the most moving scene in the film: the scene when Anton Ego gets transported back to his childhood by the taste of ratatouille. Its reference to the most famous scene in Marcel Proust's *Á la recherche du temps perdu* (*In Search of Lost Time*) is obvious – that scene in the first part ('Combray') when the narrator as a grown-up dips a *madeleine* in a cup of tea and suddenly is transported back to the moment of his childhood when he had that same sensation of taste. Also in Proust, the decisive taste is connected to maternal care: the tea and madeleine are served by the grown-up narrator's mother, and was in his childhood served to him by his aunt. Until the moment of the madeleine, the narrator's remembrance of his childhood summers has been limited to his bedroom, described as a coffin in which he had to put himself, executing his own sentence of death, when his mother could not kiss him goodnight because she and his father were occupied with their frequent guest, Mr Swann. So, both Anton Ego and the narrator in Proust are liberated from their life-in-a-coffin as they get a taste of maternal care. In a truly funny portrait of the critic in his apartment, Anton Ego is depicted as a vampire in his coffin, and the taste of ratatouille as that which takes him out of this death-in-life could be seen as an event not unlike the Christian resurrection or the gesture of love that installs a kind of new life.

To French philosopher Alain Badiou 'the event' is that which breaks into your existence and installs a 'before' and 'after', be it love, resurrection, scientific discovery, revolution or art. In Anton Ego's case the dish of ratatouille could be seen as an event of art as well as love, and he does what Badiou proscribes for those who have been struck by an event: he stays true to it, giving up his life as a vampire, following Remy, giving up judging for receiving, taking his place as a true master – the one who leaves it to others to guess his desire ('Surprise me!'). This 'conversion' is so beautifully told that I am ready to bear with the populist strain of the story: the bistro is better than the fine restaurant, Anton Ego is better as a man of the people than as an elitist critic . . .

By refining and serving the simple dish of ratatouille, Remy could be said to give something he does not have (be it human skill or maternal care) to Anton Ego who does not want it (as he takes enjoyment in blaming rather than praising, and as it will unsettle his entire existence as critic-in-the-coffin).

'Anyone can cook' – this is the outspoken dictum of the film, seemingly a very democratic, inclusive and tolerant dictum, but one that has through the film to be reinterpreted: it is not that anyone can cook, it is that someone with a talent for cooking could come from anywhere, even a family of rats. This is the liberalist version of democracy: it is not that everyone should be recognized, it is that the specially talented should be recognized from wherever he comes. In late capitalist consumers' society one could ask whether titles like this have not rather become a kind of superego commandment: You ought to cook! Yet the images of the film give us another version of the saying: anyone can cook if he lets a rat into his toque.

10

Humanity Stuck in Vacation Hell: *Wall-E*

The love story between two robots, one of them mechanical-looking like a rusty tractor and designed to collect garbage, the other one hyper-digital, aerodynamically designed in the style of a white MacBook as a probe for a spaceship. Does this sound like a possible relationship? If not, do not worry, because its very impossibility might make it the perfect image of the sexual relationship between man and woman, which is, according to Lacan, non-existent. But the impossible sexual relationship is supplemented by something called love.

Wall-E is at once a love story and a dystopia of the society of enjoyment, a poetic vision of earth as a post-apocalyptic wasteland, and a dystopian vision of the ultimate consumers' society as a totalitarian state. The two robots, Wall-E and Eve, can be seen as representing Lacan's 'masculine' and 'feminine' positions that will here be related to Kierkegaard's distinction between 'Law' and 'love'. I shall argue that *Wall-E* proposes 'love' as the antidote to that obscene imperative to enjoy to which we are subjected in late capitalist society, and which has as its utter consequence the complete entropy of enjoyment. It seems, though, that the story of salvation told in the film has in it a danger of collapsing into just a new kind of totalitarianism. As for the question of what animates the human being, this film seems to point to movie-watching (!) and the very principle of differentiation at work at the base of language and naming.

Wall-E (Andrew Stanton, 2008) is clearly divided into two parts: the first one very poetic and non-verbal, depicting earth as a wasteland of garbage after humanity has left, the second one very narrative, full of chase and dialogue, taking place on the spaceship to which humanity has been evacuated, like some Noah's Ark.

In the poetic wasteland part we see Wall-E (Ben Burtt), seemingly the only robot left on earth, moving around among heaps of garbage that he daily and thoroughly collects, presses to squares, and organizes in towers, looking like a garbage version of a city skyline. From the garbage Wall-E selects special items that he shelves in the kind of garage where he 'sleeps' – which means folds together to reload, awakening next morning to the sound of a MacBook (!) rebooting itself.

Wall-E has made a home out of his garage, not least by placing a video in it, repeatedly putting on an old Hollywood musical film with dance and love scenes (taken and partly manipulated from *Hello, Dolly*) that thoroughly fascinate him. The only living creature around Wall-E is a cockroach, appearing as some kind of indestructible, primitive life; that kind of life that persists when humanity disappears. The temporality of the wasteland is repetitive, cyclic – the only events being explosions regularly shaking the earth, but from which Wall-E has the habit of saving himself by hiding in his garage.

Then one day, Wall-E finds a small plant among the garbage, intuitively seeing it as something precious, taking it home to take care of it. And shortly after, notified by a bizarre dancing red spot of light, a spaceship lands and lets loose the slim, aerodynamic probe as if it were an egg. Wall-E is completely fascinated by the probe's gracious flying around like dancing, but as she (for a she it is, feminized by the gracious dance and Wall-E's infatuated gaze) discovers him she turns from dancer to a kind of *Kill Bill* figure, violently firing at him with her 'arm' (being an 'arm' in both senses of the word). Through their common love for the small cockroach they get reconciled, though, and the first sounds that seem like words are heard in the film when they introduce themselves to one another with their synthetic robot voices: the probe's name 'Eve' sounding a bit like a mirror figure of 'Wall-E'. Wall-E shows Eve (Elissa Knight) his home – where she bumps around like a maniac and fixes his Rubik's Cube in a split second – and in a moving scene they watch together the scene from *Hello, Dolly* when the lovers take one another's hands, imitating this gesture with the extremities of their robot arms.

As Eve discovers the small plant that Wall-E has found, though, she determinately encapsulates it and falls into what seems an unconscious slumber, brooding over the plant in her inner like a hen over her egg or a pregnant woman over her foetus. In this state she is waited upon by her lover, Wall-E, treating her like a cavalier treats his beloved, taking her sailing in a gondola or to see a beautiful view, taking care of her and protecting her from the rain, while she stays in her slumber, completely folded upon herself.

As the spaceship lands again, re-collecting Eve, and Wall-E manages to hang on to her, the second part of the film begins. Here we are in a dystopian vision of the consumer's society: humanity having lived for centuries on the spaceship has become fat and weak, sitting like adult babies, each one in his transport chair, having food and entertainment served, never having to use their bodies. In this universe the film unfolds its story of conflicts and chase around the precious object, the plant that Eve brings to evacuated humanity like the dove brings the olive branch to Noah.

When the plant is scanned, the captain is ordered by his computer (voiced by Sigourney Weaver) to go back to earth, but he finds an unexpected adversary in 'Auto', the computerized steering wheel that has certainly become autonomous, trying to prevent the mission to go back to earth. Through the efforts of Eve and Wall-E, though, and the captain's desire to know earthly matters, being inspired by the computer's illustrated encyclopaedic definitions of phenomena such as 'dance' and 'farming', the spaceship finally lands on earth, humanity taking its first insecure steps on the planet it left centuries ago. The credits at the end show a strangely touching tale of humanity developing 'once again' through pictures stylistically imitating the road of art history, from cave paintings via hieroglyphs and Renaissance drawings to Turner, Pissarro and van Gogh.

Whereas the wasteland of earth has a poetic beauty of its own, the perfect society in space is utterly disgusting: 'humanity stuck in vacation hell', as the director Andrew Stanton very precisely puts it in the commentary track. When one is confined to the sterile and shopping mall-like world of the spaceship in the second part, one truly longs for the dirt and garbage heaps of earth. Stanton also has a very interesting reflection on the relationship between the film's two stories, saying that 'the love story' has as its by-product 'the salvation of humanity'. This may sound as a complete reversal of the hierarchy that one should expect between 'love story' and 'salvation of humanity'. It does correspond, though, to my feeling that the first part of the film is by far the stronger. And it may even contain a truth about 'love' as that which could actually break through that obscene imperative to enjoy, to which we are subjected in late capitalist society, and which has as its utter consequence the complete entropy of enjoyment, as shown in the film's 'vacation hell'. I shall claim, though, that the story of salvation has in it a danger of collapsing into just a new kind of totalitarianism.

So, what is love, and what is the dystopia of enjoyment? As love is a very difficult thing to talk about – also for Lacan who mostly speaks about it in riddles, like his famous saying, 'Love is to give something you do not have to someone who does not want it' – I shall start with the dystopia of enjoyment. Then I will approach the first part and its introduction of the themes of sexual difference and love, first by showing how these themes are in *Wall-E* linked to the theme of animation, secondly by departing from a close reading of the very first scene.

Enjoy!

The development of capitalist society, from its puritan beginning to the consumer's society of today, could roughly be described as a development from duty to enjoyment. Or from the puritan commandment: man does not deserve anything, to the commandment of the commercial: you deserve this ('because you are worth it'). What is important (and often misunderstood by conservative cultural critics) is that in both cases we are dealing with commandments. It is not as if the late capitalist consumer has become 'liberated' from duty and superego, it is rather that he now has the duty to enjoy (and if he has trouble in doing so, he can have some Viagra). The superego of late capitalism tells us in shining neon letters: Enjoy!

Now, according to Lacan, superego as the commandment to enjoy is not even a new thing, but as old as the superego itself. This is what he states by coining the concept of 'the obscene superego' (Lacan 2006: 517). To Lacan, here following Melanie Klein (Klein 1998a), the superego is originally something more primitive and sadistic than the rational, socializing voice of Law and reason; rather than having its image in the reasonable, loving father it has its image in the capricious mother, something like the Mummy in Hitchcock's *Psycho*, riding the back of her son while shouting her unreasonable demands. In *Wall-E*, superego as a kind of empty, sadistic mechanics could be said to find its image in Auto, the steering wheel that has become not only automatic, but also autonomous, having his own will which is going against the official (though not commonly known) plan for the spaceship to return to earth. Auto is the steering mechanism of the superego without any aim, having detached himself from the directives giving meaning to the journey of the spaceship, his name being nothing but the naming of the non-teleological automatism of the superego. Furthermore, Auto as a big red eye is certainly also the Other (Auto/*Autre*) as cruel gaze, pointing again to the sadism of Authority (Auto/Authority).

Rather than in Kant and his moral imperative (you can do this because you must), the Lacanian superego has its image in Sade and his imperative to enjoy (you must do this because you can). The idea that duty and enjoyment are induced at the same time actually goes back to St Paul and his famous lines in Romans 7:7: 'I do not know sin, but by the law; for I had not known concupiscence, if the law did not say: Thou shalt not covet.' What Paul is saying here, is that by telling us what we cannot do, the Law at the same time tells us what we really want to do. When the Ten Commandments tell us not to steal, kill, cheat, envy, etc., they at the same time tell us that these are the really enjoyable things to do.

So this is one way that we must understand the obscenity of the superego: as the definition of enjoyable things to do by their very negation, as the prohibition ('Don't!') having as its echo the incitement which was in the age of morality a sly and whispering voice, but has now become the loud, shouting message of the commercials: 'Just do it!' Another aspect of the obscene superego is the primitive enjoyment involved in the execution of the Law that we know from public executions: *les tricoteuses* at the guillotine, the cheering crowd at the gallows, etc. In Pixar this kind of Law-as-sadistic-enjoyment may be found in *Ratatouille* in the figure of Skinner in a rage with Alfredo, screaming: 'The Law is on my side, drive him through the sausage press.' According to Žižek, with Judaism the Law moved from 'the living substance of enjoyment' into 'the dead letter', and with Kafka this movement was reversed as his stories are 'flooding the judicial domain once again with enjoyment' (Žižek 1991: 150). Yet a third way, though related to the first two, is the obscene Law as that 'secret code' that always seems to appear besides the official law, as its product as well as its support: the clandestine rites of the mariners, the Ku Klux Klan, the Mafia, etc. The tyrant regime of the teddy bear Lotso in *Toy Story 3* would be an example of such an obscene, unofficial law.

If we are living today under the imperative to enjoy, we certainly also feel the counter strike: the imperative to stay healthy, to detox, to avoid any enjoyable substance such as fat, sugar, alcohol, tobacco. In *How to Read Lacan*, Žižek (2006: 91–2) explains this tendency by the fact that God is dead. Or rather by Lacan's understanding of the consequence of God's death: 'If God doesn't exist, then nothing at all is permitted any longer' (Lacan 1988: 128). As long as we have a God telling us not to eat/smoke/fornicate, we also have the obscene imperative: Eat! Smoke! Fornicate! The very prohibition is what makes possible orgies. When God does not exist any longer, one possible solution is to render harmless that dangerous enjoyment which, as long as God existed, was allowed to be dangerous, because it was forbidden ... Thus we get food without fat, coffee without caffeine, sweets without sugar, beers without alcohol, smoking without inhaling, sex without fornicating (cybersex), and even (as in the blockbusters *Twilight* and *True Blood*) vampirism without (human) blood.

So, on the one hand, late capitalist society subjects us all to the imperative of enjoyment; on the other hand that harmful 'extra' which makes enjoyment enjoyable is removed. This is our imperative: 'It is your duty to enjoy, but we have removed the very substance of enjoyment.'

The dystopia of the evacuated humanity in *Wall-E* is the utter consequence of this imperative, this entropy of enjoyment by the very imperative to enjoy. The dystopia in *Wall-E* is not the wasteland that earth has become after some ecological catastrophe, as this wasteland has a melancholic and magical poetry of its own. The dystopia is the community of completely passive consumers, having no other duty but the duty to enjoy, and thereby having lost all enjoyment. Apparently the inhabitants of the spaceship are not eating non-fat food, but they seem to know of no dangerous 'adult' substance of enjoyment, such as drugs, sex and alcohol. The dystopia is a reality actually quite close to that which we already know on earth, whereas the vision of earth as a wasteland has another magic than the world that we know of. If the citizens on the spaceship seem to be almost unanimated, machine-like, the wasteland part tells us the story of machines becoming animated, by sexual difference and love. The recurrent Pixar theme of animation, what animates the human subject, is in *Wall-E* present as the question of the relationship between humans and machines. The dystopia of the film is about humans having become machines, and the love story is about machines becoming human.

Animation

In *Wall-E*, humans have become machines, being supplied with fuel, but knowing of no desire. The machines, on the contrary, get to know desire, and perhaps even love. So, what does animate Wall-E and Eve? What turns them from being machines into being human-like subjects?

As we have seen in other Pixar films, gaze and voice become distinctive human traits. Eve's humanization actually shows how little it takes to give the impression of 'gaze', almost as if being an experiment of minimizing the visual sign for 'human face'. The moment the two red lights on her facial screen are varied between spots and bows, we get the impression of gaze and face, showing the minimal difference it takes for something to become expressive. Or, to put it in a more Lacanian way: as soon as there is difference between two traits, they become signifiers. The difference between spot and bow is enough for Eve's eyes to become signifying, calling for our interpretation: is she angry or friendly, hostile or giggling?

Difference is also the principle that turns the sounds of the computers into voice: the differentiation of sound into phonemes, words, names. Actually the verbal word appears in *Wall-E* as name, as two names, once again in a kind of minimal differentiation: the difference between 'Wall-E' and 'Eve'. The name 'Eve' is pronounced more like 'E-va' which makes of its relation to the name of 'Wall-E' something like an echo or mirror. The subtle difference between the two names at the same time marks a sexual difference. Staging the origin of language, the scene must be said to do this in a Lacanian rather than Saussurian way. Saussure was the one to state difference as the principle of language (a sound or a word or a letter only gets to mean something by its difference to another one), but Lacan was the one to visualize this difference constitutive of language as the difference between the signs marking sexual difference: the signs for 'Men's room' and 'Ladies' room'. Lacan does this when in his essay 'L'instance de la lettre dans l'inconscient' (Lacan 2006: 416) he replaces Saussure's illustration of the verbal sign, a naturalist drawing of a tree accompanied by the word 'tree' ('arbre'), with a pictogram of two doors marked 'Gentlemen' and 'Ladies'. This is a statement that sexual difference and the difference constituting language are interrelated, just as they appear in Genesis the moment when language is no longer a question of Adam naming the animals and God naming the world, but of Adam and Eve realizing the difference between good and evil as well as their sexual difference.

So, also 'name' and 'sex' seem in *Wall-E* to found humanity. Name as constitutive of the human subject could be a way of interpreting Lacan's definition of the signifier as 'that which represents a subject for another signifier' (Lacan 1979: 207). It is by being represented by one signifier and another, and to each other, that Wall-E and Eve become human subjects, at the same time thrown into gaze and face and voice and language and sexual difference and love. A similar scene actually appears in the spaceship part when the adult babies are thrown out of their transportation chairs due to Eve's and Wall-E's disturbing behaviour. Finding themselves confused on the floor and clinging to each other's hands, a man and a woman suddenly feel the urge to introduce themselves: 'John' – 'Mary'.

As the names of Wall-E and Eve are mirroring the names of the first people in Genesis (Wall-E and Eve in Wasteland being Adam and Eve in Eden), John (John Ratzenberger) and Mary (Kathy Najimy) are names of main characters from the gospels, thus almost signalling a relation between the two scenes (and even the two parts of the film?), as the Christian understanding of the relation between the two parts of the Bible: redemptive repetition. The installation of the dynamics of language could also be said to be repeated when the captain of the spaceship is surfing the internet on his computer, being completely fascinated by the phenomena of earth which throw him from one word to another: 'define *earth*', 'define *sea*', 'define *farm*', 'define *hoedown*', 'define *dancing*'. Here the captain is re-animated, re-awakened as a human being, by being thrown into the chain of signifiers.

The two minimally different traits of Eve's eyes testify to human gaze as something based on the differentiation that turns marks into signifiers. Wall-E's gaze seems to have another character. His 'eyes', the screen on his 'face', are shaped as binoculars, causing humoristic scenes where the vision is limited to Wall-E's binocular field, but also turning into a kind of spooky spiral forms when we look into Wall-E's eyes. The whirl in Wall-E's eyes mirror the whirls of the universe, thus forming a gaze not unlike the human gaze in which we, according to Hegel, catch sight of 'the night of the world' that is the human being. Žižek glimpses this night at the beginning of Hitchcock's *Vertigo* in the whirling shapes in Kim Novak's eyes (Žižek 1991: 97). We may glimpse it in Wall-E's eyes.

The director Andrew Stanton has a nice characteristic of Wall-E in the soundtrack: 'A robot left on earth having no idea it could stop.' This may sound very robot-like, but perhaps it is actually Wall-E's first human trait, being driven by that senseless, persistent mechanics of going on that is, according to Lacan, what human desire basically is, when purified to the death drive. But Wall-E's meeting with Eve makes him stop, or change his track, as he discovers sexual difference and language. He even seems to discover love, in a twofold movement of subjecting to symbolic order and suspending it, being programmed to love by cultural codes, and discovering love by transcending the program of cultural codes. In order to study his being 'programmed', we shall now turn to a close reading of the very first scene.

The first scene

The film starts out in the universe, very sci-fi, with pictures of galaxies and space dim, gradually zooming in on earth. Actually Pixar seems to have a predilection for universal openings: thus *Toy Story 2* opens with Buzz Lightyear in space (shortly revealed to be a computer game), and *Ratatouille* opens with a TV set floating freely in the universe. This seems to quote the logo of the Universal film company, the earth globe floating in space, representing the universalizing, imperialist ambition of the film industry. As we are approaching earth, diving into the clouds, sharing the point of view of some rocket landing, a fascinating landscape is opened: from a distance looking like trees and rocks, closer in revealing itself as heaps of garbage and ruins of skyscrapers, but at the same time gaining a kind of second nature, the appearance of an underwater world of plants and fossils.

Two interesting things with a great aesthetic effect are happening on the level of sound. First, the opening scene is accompanied by the song 'Put on Your Sunday Clothes' from *Hello, Dolly*, the lyrics of which point to a world 'out there' (the 'slick town' beyond 'this hick town'). As Stanton states on the commentary track, this creates (an aesthetically efficient) tension between sci-fi image and retro musical sound. Secondly, the song shifts from universal to local sound as Wall-E is introduced and the music is no longer smooth surround sound enveloping the universe, but streaming from Wall-E's video machine in a much inferior quality. This gives the impression that Wall-E has stored something like a small fragment of the starry sky, a little piece of the music of the spheres on his video machine.

The opening sends a signal that Universal Pictures and Hollywood musicals are what dreams are made of. Again one could see this as Pixar promoting the film industry of which it is itself a part, in the role of big O: 'universal' means a film company, and our longings (for something 'out there') are implanted in us by the films we watch.

The manipulated scene from *Hello, Dolly*, with a close-up of the lovers holding hands, actually gets to play an important part in Wall-E's becoming a human subject. First it inspires him to let his one mechanical hand hold the other, thereby aspiring to subjectivity as Maurice Merleau-Ponty defines it, when he uses exactly the image of 'my right hand touching my left hand' to explain how the subject's perception is constituted by reversibility between touching and touched, perceiving and perceived (Merleau-Ponty 1968: 133–4). Secondly it inspires him to hold hands with Eve, thereby learning love from the screen in a scene that might be said to exhibit 'love' as an imitation of cultural models.

If one continues a little along the soundtrack of the film, one finds that one of the persistent traces of humanity on earth is the stupid commercial jingle, promoting 'BnL', 'Buy and Large', which seems in the film to be a complete fusion of shopping mall and government in a parodic vision surprisingly critical of late

Figure 13 Wall-E reaching for Eve's hand. From *Wall-E* (Andrew Stanton, 2008) © Pixar.

capitalism: governmental and capital power have become one. The film has a clear-sighted vision (that may seem surprising, coming from the American film industry) of consumers' society as a totalitarian society.

The jingle as leftover, as that which persists, that which will not die, is reminiscent of the refrain of 'Brazil' as used by Terry Gilliam in his wonderful dystopian film of the same name. According to Žižek, the refrain in Gilliam's film appears as 'permeated with idiotic enjoyment', 'embody[ing] the superego imperative of idiotic enjoyment' (Žižek 1991: 128) – which is surely as true for the commercial jingle left on earth in *Wall-E*. Thus the refrain is a symptom of a society doping its citizens with enjoyment, making over totalitarian brutality with happiness. But as Žižek interprets *Brazil*, the refrain is turned from an affirmative symptom into a subversive 'sinthome'.

'Sinthome' is not one of Lacan's clearest concepts, but it could be understood as an instance of the real, whereas the symptom, of course, is always symbolic. So the symptom turns into 'sinthome' the moment it is no longer a sign for anything else but itself, the moment it is released from the signifying chain, meaning nothing, but just being present. In the example of the jingle, at this moment its 'idiotic enjoyment' is no longer a symptom of an ideology turning citizens into idiots, but of a persistent will to happiness that inspires to revolt against that very ideology.

The BnL jingle in Wall-E could hardly be said to aspire to such subversive power, but the scene from *Hello, Dolly* could. Actually it is just a piece of garbage, just some leftover from the film industry, but precisely as garbage, as a fragment it might be said to have a redemptive function.

The leftover

The world as a wasteland is a post-apocalyptic, but also very baroque figure. In the dualist baroque worldview, contrary to the romantic one, the things of the world are empty of meaning, as God is not present in it. In a post-apocalyptic scenario like the one in *Wall-E*, the things of the world are without functionality, as humanity has left earth. The result is a bit the same: ridden of divine meaning or instrumental functionality, the things may take on a new meaning, as the collector lifts them up and puts them in new constellations. Wall-E this way belongs to the family of baroque melancholics, inventive allegorists, and modern collectors that put together fragments of the world's trash into new constellations and alphabets. Just like the melancholic in Walter Benjamin's understanding must dive into the soil for the garbage, the ruins, the dead objects, to see them suddenly filled with new and different meaning, like the skulls of Golgotha suddenly mean resurrection (Benjamin 1977: 232), so Wall-E finds in the garbage heaps useless objects and brings them home to his collection, suspended from meaning, but thereby gaining a new magic, a new potential for possible meanings. The idea that somehow you have to go deep down into the trash for some kind of salvation to take place is present also in the second half of the film, when Wall-E and Eve as a part of their love story have to go together deep down into the garbage chute on the spaceship.

Appearing in this wasteland, watched by a robot, the dancing scene is alienated; as spectators we are somehow decoded from our habitual perception, sharing Wall-E's point of view, understanding that what we call 'dance' may to the uninitiated look just like people moving their limbs in an unmotivated way. Yet the moment when man and woman take each other's hands has this strange attraction on Wall-E, as if transmitting the possibility of another kind of life. The gesture reappears with this function in the film's second part, when John and Mary are thrown out of their transportation chairs and suddenly find themselves holding hands, clearly depicted as some kind of awakening. The force that will finally disturb the dystopian society of the spaceship emanates from the film scene of holding hands, teaching Wall-E and Eve to do the same, thereby generating the love story that will undermine the mechanical society of the spaceship. This is not love as an escapism that allows you to ignore political problems, this is love as a revolutionary force.

Or, rather, you could look at the function of the film scene, including its auditory transformation from universal to local, from the point of view of ideology critique, seeing it as another instance of the film industry as the big, manipulating O – or, you could, more in the manner of Walter Benjamin, regard it as dream stuff from which revolutionary energy can be gained.

So the film scene could be seen as a persistent leftover, as something that does not want to die, and perhaps containing the same possible switch from 'idiotic enjoyment' to revolutionary energy. It might be seen also as the *a* in Wall-E; as 'that which is in him more than himself'. It might even be that which Wall-E, without having it, gives to Eve who does not want it, thus being a token of love, if one should listen to Lacan: 'Love is giving something you do not have to someone who does not want it.' As something exterior and strange to Wall-E, he cannot be said to 'have' the image of holding hands, and even if she is curious to watch and imitate the image, it is not that Eve really wants it. What Eve really wants is the plant, which is the second important leftover in the film. The third one is the cockroach.

The cockroach is clearly an instance of that which does not want to die, and thus in Lacanian terms an instance of 'the real', understood as that life which transgresses and survives the forms of human existence. Interestingly it is the cockroach that unites Eve and Wall-E at first; in their common liking of the small creature they stop fighting, or rather Eve stops shooting at Wall-E.

As for the plant, it seems to have a double function of support and revolt, not unlike the film scene. On the one hand it is related to Eve's directive; she is programmed to want the plant, and thus her desire seems a perfect illustration of one of Lacan's definitions of desire: 'Desire is the Other's desire.' Eve's desire has literally been put into her by the big O, aka spaceship society. On the other hand, though, the plant is a gift of love from Wall-E to Eve and even pollutes her. Around the plant the story evolves from a mission for the spaceship into a mission against the spaceship, as the plant turns from being what society tells Eve to want into being the dirty intrusion of Wall-E and his world into her sterile purity. The object of desire, concerting with the existing order, turns into a token of love, revolting against the existing order. The same thing that you desire in complete accordance with your social programming could suddenly turn into that which disturbs your accordance with social order. One might perhaps even read the plant as a kind of pivotal axis for the dialectical switch of desire into love: the object of desire and the token of love may be the very same thing, but having completely different functions: fitting into your inner as society has designed it (desire), or on the contrary being something foreign intruding you (love). Due to the intervention of love, the plant becomes a sign of revolution. But from here it actually undergoes a third transformation, as the sign of revolution becomes a totalitarian logo. As all signs on the spaceship towards the end change into showing 'green plant', it looks suspiciously like just another repressive system; the disturbing element and event has been transformed into the official, uniform and all-pervasive sign, like we know it from the logos of totalitarian regimes as well as of global companies.

The film's different central objects could be understood from Žižek's definition of three types of objects noted in Lacanese: $S(\not{A})$, Φ, *a* (Žižek 1991: 133–40).

$S(\not{A})$ is the signifier of the lack of the symbolic order and defined by Žižek as a 'unique' and anal, excremental object, a leftover of the real. The cockroach and the plant (as dirt and as an instance of 'the real' as that which does not want to die) could be said to have this character.

a is, as we know, the object-cause of desire, and the film scene from *Hello, Dolly* certainly has the function of being both that which causes Wall-E's desire and designates an object for this desire. The plant, as I have tried to show, travels between being an excremental leftover of the real, and having the function of *a* (Eve's object of desire, and later the captain's).

Φ, in opposition to *a*, is the surplus-object, the object signifying nothing, the stain. One of Žižek's clear examples of this kind of object is the birds in Hitchcock's film of the same name, or the enormous redwood tree in *Vertigo*: objects with a mighty presence, but no signification. The BnL jingle could be said to be an object of this kind, having lost any meaning, but just being there. Another possible candidate for this object function in *Wall-E* is the steering wheel Auto seen as a red gaze, a stain in our visual field, being all 'Auto', not referring to any order or meaning, but just to his own mechanical will.

Man and woman

Translated into the sexual relation between man and woman, the story of the plant is the story of woman desiring a child, while man desires woman (or that unfathomable *je-ne-sais-quoi* that he finds emanating from woman). (This would be one way to understand the 'impossibility' of the sexual relation as Lacan claims it: there is just no reciprocity in man's and woman's desire.) Thus Wall-E's giving the plant to Eve could surely be read as an insemination, and the beauty of the story is that it is at the same time a pollution. In fulfilling her desire Eve has let in some dirt that slowly transforms her from being just a desiring machine into leaving her life-as-machine out of love.

The first consequence of Eve's insemination, though, is her falling into that death-like slumber which may be seen as the pregnant woman closing herself upon the life in her womb. A state of depression, one might call it, if this means also 'the depressive position' as defined by Melanie Klein: a state of brooding also in the creative sense of folding onto oneself in order to collect and contain all kinds of partial and fragmented objects (Klein 1998b, 1998c). By changing completely from her manic state of playing and dancing, threatening almost to destroy Wall-E's garage by her uninhibited conduct, into the depressive state of brooding upon her plant, Eve seems to represent woman as some kind of manic-depressive – an image of woman that we know from the cowgirl Jessie in *Toy Story 2*, and that will recur in another Pixar film, *Up*, as Fredericksen's wife is switching between the position of a manic girl and the position of the depressive woman (in her case depressive for not being pregnant).

From the masculine point of view, that is from Wall-E's point of view, Eve's 'depressive' state is a mystery, and his relation to the slumbering Eve becomes a precise, partly touching, partly comical image of man's relation to woman. Besides the well-known figure of Woman-as-depressive, Eve is, in all her impressive, aerodynamic technicality, of course also the well-known figure of Woman-as-cyborg. In both cases she is a mystery to man, wanting either to wake her up from her depression or open her up to see how she works. Woman-as-cyborg seems to be prefigured in Wall-E finding a bra and putting it on as a pair of glasses – this kind of masculine 'how does this work' attitude to feminine accessories or body parts, reminiscent of the scene in *Vertigo* when James Stewart examines the bra on his designer friend's table and learns from her that its system is designed by a constructor of planes. Director Stanton beautifully supports this image of woman as complicated technology on the commentary track when comparing Wall-E to a tractor and Eve to a Porsche or another advanced machine: 'You don't understand how it works, but it has a logic.' Feminine logic, that is . . .

As for the depressive, mysterious Eve, Wall-E partly watches lovingly over her, partly wants to awaken her. Like a romantic lover he takes her round, to watch a beautiful view, to be her gondolier while decorating her with coloured bulbs.

This clearly has a comic dimension to it: woman as the unconscious thing that man carries around and stages in different settings (the crude association is the plastic life-size sex doll). It also has something very touching about it, though, as if Wall-E is carefully 'holding' Eve while she is 'holding' her plant/child – the word 'holding' here to be taken in the sense of object relation theory as that caring embrace, mental as well as physical, that enables the other to collect and contain his fragments and parts. The touching dimension is reinforced when later, on the spaceship, Eve watches Wall-E's memories from that period – being stored on his inner video tape, which is, in this world of human machines, not a metaphor, but an actual tape, giving Eve the concrete opportunity to see the world with her lover's eyes, making her realize how he has been watching over her all the time while she was in her unconscious slumber.

Comical or touching, the scenes of Wall-E watching over his unconscious Eve certainly also have a philosophical dimension, giving us an image of woman not unlike that of Isabella Rossellini's character (Dorothy) in David Lynch's *Blue Velvet*. In Žižek's interpretation of this film, Rossellini is not being depressed because Dennis Hopper's sadistic character (Frank) is mistreating her; on the contrary, Dennis Hopper is mistreating her in order to wake her up from her depression. At the same time Žižek regards this depressive feminine position as the foundation of the subject, as that 'night of the world' (Hegel) which is at the core of subjectivity, thus claiming 'femininity' to be the model for universal subjectivity, rather than 'masculinity' as feminist critics would have it (Žižek 1994: 121–2). Disappearing into her 'night of the world', Eve could be seen as representing this founding feminine position of the subject, while all of Wall-E's activities are masculine attempts to wake her up.

The sexuation graph

In seminar XX Lacan formalizes the positions of 'man' and 'woman' in his scheme of 'sexuation'. Sexuation means taking on (mostly unconsciously) a gendered position. To Lacan, the positions of 'man' and 'woman' are positions in the symbolic order, that is positions that we take when entering into the social and linguistic order, thus being not necessarily correlative to the biological sex. Thus the masculine position, $\$$, is also the position of the hysteric – who is prototypically a biological woman. And the feminine position, S(Ⱥ), is also the position of the mystic, whether male or female. '$\$$' means the split subject, the subject that has

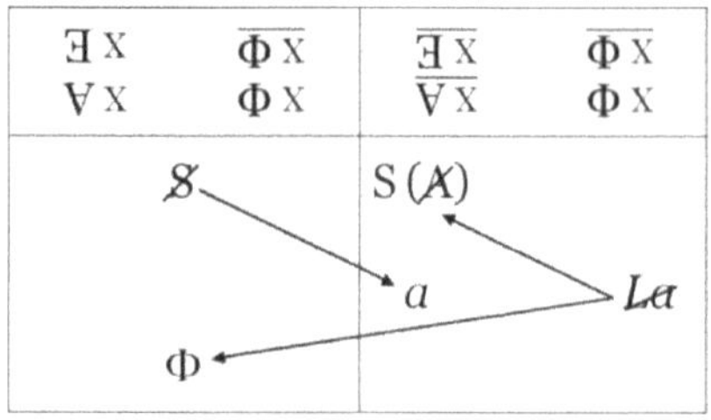

Figure 14 Lacan's sexuation graph.

entered the symbolic order (the order of society and language) through symbolic castration, that is through that 'cut' which separates child from mother, thing from word, boy from girl, old from young, conscious from unconscious, the desiring subject from its desired object (thereby generating desire at all). The line across the 'S' marks this cut. In the feminine position the cut does not run through the 'S' (the signifier of the subject), but through the 'A', the signifier of *l'Autre*, the big Other, the instance 'supposed to know' how we should lead our lives. Ultimately functioning as our big Other is the symbolic order itself, that is the rules and conventions of society and language that define our position in the world, for instance our positions as 'men' or 'women'. Thus the line across the 'A' could be understood as a cut or lack in the symbolic order, as that which is not contained in the symbolic order, that for which there is no word in language or no well defined place in society. The feminine position is in two ways defined by this lack: on the one hand the very feminine position is a 'lack' in the (patriarchal) sociolinguistic order that basically defines its subjects as masculine (that is, 'castrated'), while on the other hand the feminine position has a kind of communion with this lack, with something that escapes language. Think of the holy Theresa in orgasmic communion with God, Mary in communion with the Holy Spirit, or the witch in communion with Satan. Even think of the space probe Eve in some kind of secret communion with the plant in her inner, in a state beyond consciousness and language. Or think of Stanton's remark about Eve: she has a logic, but you don't understand how it works. Some kind of 'other logic', just as Lacan speaks of this kind of 'other enjoyment' of the feminine position, other than the logic and enjoyment of masculine desire.

What complicates things on the feminine side is the other notation of the feminine position: the 'La' under erasure. This means that *La* Femme, *The* Woman, does not exist. 'Woman' in definite singular, Woman with a capital 'W', is the fantasy of a feminine essence ('das ewig-Weibliche' as Goethe called it) that does not exist.

But still, like the unconscious, she insists. The two arrows pointing from her to the feminine subject S(Ⱥ) and to the phallus on the masculine side seem to indicate that her desire takes for its object either the masculine phallus (for instance the social status, the property, or the child that she may wish from man) or the position of being in communion with something exceeding the symbolic order.

Masculine desire is 'desire' as generally defined by Lacan: the desire being installed by the Law which at the same time defines and prohibits your object of desire ('Do not eat the apple from the tree of knowledge'). In Lacan's sexuation scheme the split, masculine subject ($) directs itself towards the little *a* (the object of desire) which is to be found on the feminine side. This could be roughly understood as a way to notate woman as man's object of desire, but it is more subtle than this if one bears in mind Lacan's definition of object *a* as 'that which is in you more than yourself'. This gives us the image of man desiring that in woman which is in her more than herself, whether one calls it 'femininity', 'mystery', 'sex appeal' or simply 'it': 'she's got *it*'.

One might see Eve's desire for the plant as woman's desire for (the child as) phallus. Once fertilized, she finds herself in the position of S(Ⱥ), at first representing (for Wall-E) the feminine mystery, later connecting to the lack of the symbolic order (understood as that which has been left out of the spaceship society). She is no longer desiring the plant as her little *a*; she now has the little *a* inside her ('that which is in you more than you'). And this little *a* inside her makes of woman the mystery to man, wanting somehow to open her up in an attempt to find it, which is exactly what Wall-E does at a moment on the spaceship.

So, the depressive position would be one way to actualize the feminine position of S(Ⱥ); woman being completely absorbed by something in herself, whether a lack or something 'more than herself', anyway something beyond words. The manic position may be another way; woman here also dealing with something that exceeds the symbolic order, even if in this case this 'something' is rather some pure, excessive energy than an inner lack or an excessive inner object. To put it in other words: the depressive woman as well as the maenad could be understood as variations of S(Ⱥ); woman is both the lacking and the excessive one in relation to the order of language and society, which might explain the manic-depressive character of the typical Pixar feminine position.

So far, we have only talked about the lower part of the sexuation scheme. The mathematical notations of the upper part means: there is one who is not castrated, everyone is castrated (masculine position); there is no one who is not castrated, non-all is castrated (feminine position). Basically this means that man is subjected to the fantasy of the one exception from the Law, the one who is not castrated (as the primal father of the tribe in Freud's myth is the founding exception to the Law, the one who can eat, kill and fornicate with no restrictions), while in the feminine position there is no such one exception from the law, but then again castration is non-all; there is something (in each subject) that escapes castration. As for the masculine fantasy of the one exception to the Law, one should think of Freud's myth ('Totem and Taboo') of the primal father or the father-of-enjoyment: the one who could eat and kill and fornicate with no restrictions, until he was killed by his jealous sons who then felt so guilty that this guilt became the very force of their founding and submitting to the Law. This is what the two seemingly paradoxical lines on the masculine side signify: there is one x who is not castrated (the primal father is exempted from the Law), everyone is castrated (all the sons have submitted to the Law). One could also put it like this: the submission under the Law implies the fantasy of the primal father. The lawful citizen, the one with a strong superego, will always have the fantasy of a position of uninhibited enjoyment. He may for instance call this position 'woman', imagining woman (as Freud) to have no superego or (as Lacan) to have an enjoyment of her own escaping Law and order. On the feminine there is no 'one' exception, but this makes of all of us exceptions, as the exception from castration has become a part of each subject, instead of being relegated to the fantasy of one (primal father or Woman) completely beyond castration.

The 'non-all' is one of Lacan's very important notations and one that can keep you philosophizing for years. Žižek uses it for, among other things, criticizing both the position of scientific materialism (biologism) and what he calls 'discursive materialism' (constructivism). Those are today the two dominant and opposite positions when it comes to defining the masculine and the feminine: either as biologically determined or as culturally, linguistically constructed positions. It seems as if 'there are only bodies and languages', as Alain Badiou puts it. But to a philosophy inspired by psychoanalysis there is more. Thus Badiou's complete statement goes like this: 'There are only bodies and languages. Except that there are truths' (Badiou 2013: 4). To biologism, the body is all. To constructivism, language is all. To the third position, which Žižek calls dialectic or even 'true' materialism, body as well as language is non-all. Which is something different from 'not all'. The 'not all' position would include the idea of the exception that you find on the masculine side of the sexuation scheme, whereas the non-all is on the feminine side. Thus metaphysics is based on the idea that 'material reality is not all', posing some kind of spiritual exception that has founded material reality (structurally the same position as the uncastrated father in Freud's myth of the primal tribe). Dialectical materialism, on the other hand, poses material reality as 'non-all', that is the substance of the world as imperfect, always including a void, some kind of 'fuzzy proto-reality' as Žižek calls it (Žižek 2009: 95).

Thus, on the feminine side you find nothing less than truth. But there is another way to understand it: what you find is a patriarchal fantasy of woman. This is to me the irreducible ambivalence of the sexuation scheme: does it picture the patriarchal symbolic-imaginary order on the masculine side (the 'Law' of symbolic castration, including the fantasy of an uncastrated position), and the truth of the real (that which exceeds the big Other: Ⱥ) on the feminine side? Or is the feminine side rather a fantasy produced by the patriarchal order? When Lacan states that, 'Woman is one name of the father', 'Woman' is actually just another version of the primal father, the symbolically castrated subject's fantasy of an uncastrated position (the femme fatale, the woman with no superego, etc.). When the feminine side is defined as 'nothing but exceptions' this could also sound like a masculine, Don Juanistic view of women as each of them 'very special', which finally means being just another one in the row. When a man tells a woman 'you are very special', this is when she should be really worried.

In a beautiful image from *Wall-E* Eve is being suspended on a row with other probes exactly like her, but being distinguished by the little green flash that shows the plant inside her – thus confirming the Don Juanistic paradox that the desired woman is at once just one in the row and something very special, as 'she's got *it*'. But the next moment it will be another one in the row who has got it.

Law and love

If you do not read it as a fantasy of the (patriarchal) Law (masculine side), the feminine position could be read as that which actually transcends the logic of that Law.

The masculine side of the scheme depicts a subject submitted to the Law and includes the two important Lacanian points about the logic of the Law: the upper part tells us that subjection to the Law implies the fantasy of the primal father, and the lower part tells us that desire is born with the Law, by indicating the direction of the split (symbolically castrated, socially initiated) subject ($) towards the object of desire (*a*).

The feminine side of the scheme, on the other hand, designates a position not completely submitted to the Law, having to do with a lack in the Law or with something exceeding it. This something might be called 'love'.

Thus, as well as being a scheme of 'man' and 'woman', the sexuation scheme is a scheme of 'Law' and 'love' as Kierkegaard defines those in *Works of Love*. This is how it has been read by Slavoj Žižek and Alain Badiou. The feminine position is understood as the position of love, because it is beyond phallic logic of desire, it is related to the real (the lack in the symbolic), and it dismisses the fantasy of the primal father. Love is about sharing the lack/the gap and not trying to fill it out by means of the other or by some fantasy of perfect love.

Somehow Eve and Wall-E watching *Hello, Dolly* together seems to me a touching image of 'love'. You might say that Hollywood here functions as their big O, telling them what to desire. But you might also see them as two clumsy creatures sharing their alienation in front of the mirror image.

Put in another way: you might read *Wall-E* as a story in which the relationship between the two robots awakes the law of desire needed to escape the state of death-like enjoyment into which humanity has sunk. But you might also read it as a story of love (feminine position) breaking through the law of desire (masculine position) which has as its ultimate consequence the complete entropy of desire, as the (consumerist) imperative to enjoy finally does away with all obstacles to enjoyment.

Thus the sexuation scheme might teach us something about Wall-E and Eve (or Wall-E and Eve might teach us something about the sexuation scheme). Even more important, though, it might teach us something about the relation between the dystopia and the love story of *Wall-E*, about love as a way to save a humanity subjected to a Law in which enjoyment has imploded, or, as director Stanton puts it: stuck in vacation hell.

11

His Master's Voice: *Up*

With *Up* we return to the theme of the voice introduced in the analysis of *Toy Story*. In *Up* the voice is clearly presented as that which humanizes the animal, when in the film's second part we meet a group of talking dogs. Actually, the dogs have voices, because their master Muntz, the villain of the film, has put electronic necklaces around their necks, 'translators', that enable them to talk. This sends us back to the idea of the voice as an alien, expressed in Žižek's dictum: 'Humanity means: the alien is controlling our animal bodies.'

In his book *The Voice in Cinema*, the French film theorist Michel Chion has pointed to the split between voice and body as a feature of cinematic art and its history: in the era of the silent movies the bodies on the screen had no voices, and even now their voices actually emanate from another place, so that the spectator has to create the perceptive illusion of the voices as emanating from the screen.

This chapter will focus on the theme and function of voice in *Up*, inspired by Chion's reflections and his concept of the *acousmêtre* (voice without a body). The dogs' voices are actually their master's invention, in a kind of subtle visual pun on the dog listening to 'His Master's Voice' in the famous advertisement picture (from the record label HMV). In the film, the theme of 'his master's voice' is further related to shame. What is the relation between master, voice and shame? This shall be discussed through Lacan's concept of the big Other. On the one hand the dogs are presented as Pavlov's dogs, animated by conditioned stimulus; on the other hand they are, through the theme of 'his master's voice', presented as animated by their master's desire. Or, as Lacan would have it: the dogs are drooling from Pavlov's desire. What makes us drool, what animates us? Are we animals, animated by conditioned stimulus? Or are we, like the dogs in *Up*, humanized by our alien voices and our master's desire?

Up (Pete Docter, Bob Peterson, 2009) tells the story of the balloon salesman Carl Fredericksen (Edward Asner) and the two great adventures of his life, the first one his long marriage with his beloved Ellie, the second one his travel as a widower, by multicoloured balloon-driven floating house, to the goal of their common longing: the magnificent 'Paradise Falls' in South America.

We meet Carl as he and Ellie, as young children, first meet each other through their common passion for adventures and explorers, notably the famous Charles Muntz (Christopher Plummer) who has discovered Paradise Falls, but has been accused of presenting a fake skeleton of a huge bird. The story of their happy marriage is told in a musical montage of snapshots during the first ten minutes of the film, showing a happy, loving couple sharing everything: interior decorating, picnicking, cleaning, car-driving, saving coins for the travel of their dreams, grieving their childlessness, but getting on, until Ellie finally dies from old age.

After Ellie's death Carl becomes an old, grumpy man, his grumpiness stressed by the fact that he is all made of squares: square face, square glasses, square body, square hands. We see him sitting sour and bitter on the porch of his multicoloured house, the home of his happy marriage, which is the only one left in a construction field. As he is sentenced to move to a retirement home, for hurting a construction worker with his walker, he ties thousands of multicoloured balloons to his house and goes up, heading for Paradise Falls. It turns out that he is not alone, though the boy scout Russell (Jordan Nagai), who has offered him his services in order to get his 'helping the elderly' badge, is clinging to the porch of the floating house.

This very odd travel company, the grumpy old man with his walker and the non-stop-talking boy scout, land in the rocky landscape of Paradise Falls. Here they meet the talking dogs, and the plot evolves around a huge multicoloured bird that Muntz and his dogs have been chasing for decades, because (as we know from the opening scene) a skeleton from this kind of bird caused his degradation as he presented it at home and was accused of fraud. Russell gets attached to the bird and calls it 'Kevin', even though it treats him maternally, and actually turns out to be a mother. One of the dogs, 'Dug' (Bob Peterson), chooses (the reluctant) Fredericksen as his new master and turns against the other dogs, led by the Doberman pinscher Alpha (also voiced by Bob Peterson) who due to a technical problem has a high, ridiculous Mickey Mouse voice.

Muntz, at first welcoming the guests on board his Zeppelin airship with great hospitality, turns out to be a villain, absorbed by his hatred for the bird who ruined his career. Fredericksen definitively takes action when in a moving scene he browses Ellie's album and discovers the small message that she has left for him after the long chronological row of photos from their married life: 'Thank you for the adventure, now go have a new one.' Through a lot of chasing and a final great battle between the two old men, Fredericksen conquers Muntz and rescues the bird, but loses his house, which disappears into the sky.

Fredericksen and Russell return home in Muntz's Zeppelin, bringing Dug. Back home Fredericksen takes on the role of Russell's absent father, attaching to his belt his 'Ellie badge' (made from a grape soda capsule) at the senior explorer ceremony, sitting on the kerb eating ice cream while counting cars (as Russell has told him he used to do with his father). The epilogue presents us with yet another photo album: Fredericksen, Russell and Dug on different excursions, having fun together as a small family.

The split of voice and body

The voice is actually highlighted from the start of the film. It opens with the scene of Carl as a young boy in the cinema in the 1930s, completely absorbed by his hero, the adventurer Charles Muntz, who is on 'Movietown News.' The images of Muntz (and Carl watching Muntz) are accompanied by a typical agitated 1930s news-reporter voice telling the story of Muntz's degradation as the huge skeleton he has brought back from his expedition to Paradise Falls is accused of being a fraud. At the end of the reportage we hear Muntz's own agitated voice, speaking from a rostrum to a large crowd of people: 'I promise to capture the beast alive, and I will not come back until I do.' His gestures, his moustache, the enthusiastic crowd, the 1930s – all of this gives to his amplified voice the connotations of a dictator's voice. As Carl has left the cinema (in a sliding cut which fixates his ravished, boyish face while changing the background from projector-lit cinema to sunlit pavement), the voice-over from the news continues, reporting Muntz's movements which Carl imitates in his play: 'He hurdles Pikes Peek, he hurdles Grand Canyon, he hurdles Mount Everest.' Thus Carl's play seems animated by a voice, the agitated reporter's voice, while Muntz's voice is introduced as a master's, even a dictator's, voice.

In *The Voice in Cinema*, Michel Chion reminds us that voice had a disappointing or even comic effect as it was introduced in cinema. Greta Garbo and other actors known from silent movies did not have the voices that people expected. Thus the actual voice was a disappointment compared with the voice in the spectators' fantasy: 'Once heard in reality even the most divine voice has something trivial about it' (Chion 1999: 9). This is the voice as the object of (the spectator's) desire, the *objet petit a*, the actualization of which is always disappointing, compared with the fantasy.

In *Up*, the discrepancy between the Doberman Alpha's frightening appearance and his Mickey Mouse voice has a comic effect not unlike what happened when the audience heard the actors' voices for the first time.

In animation films the silent movie, as discussed in this book's first chapter, seems to have partly survived. Even after the talkie had made its entrance, animation films could still be silent and even continue the slapstick style of the silent movie. In *Up*, the whole fast-forward powerful summary of Carl and Ellie's marriage is without speech. But actually it seems to be a mixture of two different speechless genres: the pantomime and the silent movie. The scenes testifying to the married couple's happiness are like pantomime; we neither see nor hear the characters talk, they express themselves by their acts, poses, mimicry and gests. Here voice is not lacking: the language without words seems to be a valid or even more valid expression of happy love. Only two scenes are like a silent movie, that is, we see the characters speak (move their lips), but we do not hear what they are saying. This is the scene when Ellie and Carl are lying in the grass and looking up at the clouds in the sky, telling each other what they think they look like, and the scene when Ellie is sitting depressed at the doctor's. Here voice is present as a lack, just as the scenes actually tell about the lack in Carl and Ellie's life, the lack of a child. In the cloud scene, the clouds turn into little babies, as we see them through Carl and Ellie's imagination, thus the baby is introduced as *objet petit a*. In the scene at the doctor's we can deduce that the couple receive the news that Ellie cannot have any children, so the desire of a child turns into a permanent lack of a child.

The voice without body

Chion's main point of interest is actually not the body without that voice which may then become a fantasmatic *objet petit a*, but the voice without a body, the *acousmêtre* as Chion calls it: the acoustic being. In his analysis of Hitchcock's *Psycho* (Chion 1992) he shows how the phenomenon of the *acousmêtre* is the driving force of the whole plot. We hear the voice of Norman Bates's mother, that cruel, sadistic superego voice of an old woman, and our narrative desire becomes the desire to discover the body from which this voice emanates. The satisfaction of this desire is horrible: the body of the voice turns out to be the mummy that turns its non-face towards us in one of film history's most famous horror scenes.

The *acousmêtre*, this bodiless voice, has a special power that Chion actually divides into four special powers: 'The powers are four: the ability to be everywhere, to see all, to know all, and to have complete power. In other words: ubiquity, panopticism, omniscience, and omnipotence' (Chion 1999: 24). The bodiless voice is ubiquitous, because we cannot localize it to one single point, and thus feel surrounded by it. It is panoptic, because of a basic paranoid mechanism in our consciousness: the one whom I cannot see, is watching me. The omniscience and omnipotence follow from the ubiquity and panopticism. Chion points to the fact that God appears as an *acousmêtre*, as pure voice, in all monotheist religions. One might even wonder if the prohibition against picturing God (in Judaism and Islam) has the function of preserving the power of the *acousmêtre*, knowing that only the voice with no body can be ubiquitous and omnipotent.

With a Lacanian term, the *acousmêtre* is the big Other, the subject supposed to know (everything), the instance watching me always and everywhere, also when I am all by myself. One might say that Chion treats the voice both as *objet petit a* (the never-satisfying object of desire) and as A (the omnipotent *acousmêtre*).

Chion proposes that the *acousmêtre* 'takes us back to an archaic, original stage: of the first months of life or even before birth, during which the voice was everything and it was everywhere [. . .] The greatest Acousmêtre is God – and even farther back, for everyone of us, the Mother' (Chion 1999: 27).

If and when the *acousmêtre* finds a body, it most often loses its power. Chion speaks of 'de-acousmatization' and points to the clearest example from film history: the last scene of *The Wizard of Oz* in which the great wizard, whose voice emanates from behind the curtain, is revealed to be a small, funny guy speaking into a microphone while he mechanically creates effects of sound and smoke (Chion 1999: 28). In Lacanian terms this is the moment when the big Other is revealed to be just an illusion, or as Lacan states: 'There is no Other of the Other' (Lacan 1998: 81). This is what Dorothy realizes at the end of *The Wizard of Oz*: 'For Dorothy this de-acousmatization marks the end of her initiation, this moment when she mourns the loss of parental omnipotence and uncovers the mortal and fallible Father' (Chion 1999: 29).

In *Up* the *acousmêtre* appears twice. In the childhood scene in the beginning, Ellie actually makes her entrance as an *acousmêtre*. As Carl is walking the pavement (or rather hurdling Pikes Peek, Grand Canyon and Mount Everest), the voice-over continuing from Movietown News is suddenly doubled by a loud and agitated girl's voice: 'Adventure is out there!' The voice-over, itself a voice without a body, is thus taken over by another *acousmêtre*, emanating from an abandoned, shabby house, and Carl goes looking for the voice's body, which turns out to be a small girl dressed in the same explorer's goggles and helmet as Carl, pretending the house is Charles Muntz's Zeppelin, agitating its 'steering wheel' while shouting and screaming excitedly. When she discovers Carl, she shouts and screams at him, her angry face with missing teeth completely up front. Here the *acousmêtre* does not really lose its power from being embodied, but the fact that Ellie appears at first as a bodiless voice seems to emphasize her role as the one who takes command of Carl's life for the next several decades.

Ellie's shrill, pervasive voice seems to be a mark of that invasive, offensive style which characterizes a certain maniac girl type in Pixar. As she removes her goggles and helmet to reassure the shocked and totally silent Carl ('Hey, I don't bite'), her red spiky hair makes her look like a small monster. She is an uninhibited (but welcomed) intruder into the silent Carl's intimate space. Her offensive intimacy continues in the scene when at night she totally shocks him by climbing through the window into his bedroom (where he is lying to recover from the broken arm she has caused), telling him that she has something to show him. In an improvised tent, made from Carl's blanket, she announces: 'I am about to let you see something that I have never shown to another human being – ever, in my life!' and Carl looks terrified, as many a small boy would be by this kind of announcement from a small, exhibitionist girl . . . What she shows him, though, is finally, not her genitals, but her adventure book, into which she has glued pictures of Charles Muntz, South America and Paradise Falls ('I ripped this right out of a library book', she tells Carl, who is once again shocked). A kind of sexual excitement is thus transferred from genitals to the adventure book, like the dream of the adventure will later replace the dream of the child (the product of genital sex) as Ellie is shown to be infertile.

The second *acousmêtre* appears when Carl Fredericksen, now an old man, and Russell are striving their way through the rocky landscape of Paradise Falls and suddenly hear a voice: 'Hey, are you okay over there?' As they (and the spectator) search for a body for this voice, a shadowy, grey, human-like figure seems to stand out from the rocks, and Fredericksen addresses him. Chion writes that just like the human figure structures visual space, so the human voice structures acoustic space. That is, we will search for a human figure in order to organize our space visually, and for a human voice in order to organize our space acoustically. Here for a moment, the structuring of visual and acoustic space seems to coincide when the human voice is located in the human-like figure. But as Fredericksen and Russell are approaching the 'human' figure, it splits in two, revealing itself to be a rock, or actually two rocks. Instead of the desired union between voice and body we get a splitting of the (only apparently) human figure. This is a radical variation of Chion's de-acousmatization. For a moment, when still at a distance, the tall, faceless, human-like shadow seems to embody the omnipresent voice that gives to it the aura of some kind of god. But when we approach it, it loses both its godlikeness and its voice. Instead we get a split figure, a splitting or castration of the big Other.

The confusion between rock and human figure triggers a kind of Rorschach perspective on every rock, not unlike the scene from the marriage montage in which Carl and Ellie are finding figures in the clouds. In a figure of inversion, another rock turns out to be actually a living dog. The question of animation is at stake: the apparently animated turns out to be inanimate, the apparently inanimate turns out to be animated. Fredericksen shouts out to the omnipresent voice: 'We have your dog', but it turns out that the voice actually belongs to the dog. This is revealed when the dog responds to Russell's tentative orders: 'Sit!' (the dog sits), 'Shake!' (the dog gives his paw), 'Speak!' – the dog says 'Hi, there!'

The dog is drooling from Pavlov's desire

Here we have the film's very remarkable and interesting image of voice as animating power: the voice is applied to the dog through an electronic necklace, a kind of 'translator' of the dog's interior monologue. As the voice humanizes the dogs, at the same time it corresponds perfectly to Žižek's definition of the voice as an alien, and humanity as 'the alien controlling our human body'. The strangeness of the voice, the voice as an alien organ, is further stressed by the fact that the dogs do not move their mouths as they speak. The fact that the voice is given to the dog by his master, that it is actually 'his master's voice', points to voice as something induced in us by the big Other, a response to the big Other's question: 'Che Vuoi?' (See this book's introduction.)

As a response to Russell's order ('Speak!') the dog's speaking voice is aligned with the other responses as conditioned reflex. This seems to confirm behaviourist theory, Dug having been conditioned, like Pavlov's dogs, to produce certain responses to certain stimuli. This theme recurs when the whole pack of dogs regularly responds to the words 'Squirrel' or 'Treat' by becoming all excited. 'Conditioned stimuli' is one, mechanist, answer to the question: 'What animates the subject?' Man is a human dog, a kind of animal machine. But in the image of the voice as that which animates us, and is at the same time an alien, we get quite another answer: man is an animal body animated (humanized) by an alien which puts him in constant dialogue with the big Other. One could also say that there are two different ways, both represented in the film, to understand the idea that the subject is animated by his master's voice: one is mechanical, the subject is conditioned by a master; the other one is psychoanalytical: the subject is born from a dialogue with the big Other, which induces into him a speaking voice like some kind of alien.

Pavlov's experiments are based on the dogs' need, their hunger. The conditioned stimulus (the ringing bell) produced salivation because it was associated with food. But by having a speaking voice and entering into dialogue with the big Other the dogs in *Up* exceed the logic of need and enter into the logic of desire.

The only desire at stake in Pavlov's experiments is, to Lacan, Pavlov's own. It is Pavlov's desire that makes the dogs drool. 'There is no other subject here than the subject of the experimenter' (Lacan 1979: 228). Pavlov is the one to get satisfaction from the experiment. To Lacan, Pavlov actually does not prove anything about the functioning of the dog's brain, but about the functioning of the signifier. The ringing bell is a signifier, and Pavlov's domesticated dogs learn to respond to this signifier by the principle of equivalence (ringing bell is equivalent of food), but not by the principle of deference and difference (Derrida's 'différance'), that is the dynamics of the signifying chain of human language.

In her wonderful essay 'Love Me, Love My Dog: Psychoanalysis and the Animal/Human Divide', Renata Salecl tells about the Russian performance artist Kulik who exhibits himself as a dog, crawling around naked on the gallery's floor, wearing a dog's necklace tied to a chain. Kulik even once played Pavlov's dog, in order to encourage the study of the psychology of animals. His idea was to propagate a new symbiosis between human and animal, a new 'zoocentrism' in which man is regarded as 'a subculture in the larger whole of the noosphere (derived from noos, the ability to smell, to feel)' (quotes from Kulik's catalogue for his 1996 Rotterdam show, Salecl 2000: 107).

In one of its first lines, still in the state of an *acousmêtre*, the dog in *Up* actually refers to its sense of smell: 'I can smell you.' But as soon as this sense of smell is verbalized, it exceeds the 'noospheric' and enters into the linguistic sphere of the human subject. Salecl insists with Lacan on the distinction between those spheres; she insists that the distinction between man and dog must be maintained, despite the wish to deconstruct it that we find in constructivist and deep ecologist trends of thought.

Exactly by playing the dog, Kulik actually, despite his intention, makes the human/animal divide very clear. As Salecl argues, he will probably never get dogs to watch his show. Whereas he himself is 'in desperate need for the audience, the gallery or, in general, the big Other. Kulik, like his predecessor Diogenes, finds enjoyment in posing as a dog only when others observe him.' The dog, on the contrary, does not relate to the big Other; it has a certain self-sufficiency that Kulik and other animal-lovers desire, but 'it may be harder for humans to learn self-sufficiency from dogs than for dogs to learn language' (Salecl 2000: 115).

In seminar IX, Lacan actually speaks of a dog that speaks, his own dog Justine. But his point is that she only speaks to him when she needs it, due to some inner pressure. When she addresses herself to him, he never has the function of the Other. As a domesticated dog, Lacan's Justine to some degree lives in language, but without the big Other. As Salecl puts it: 'The dog is in language, but it does not relate to the chain of signifiers – the big Other' (Salecl 2000: 111).

The subject is animated by the chains of signifiers and her dialogue with the big Other rather than by the instinct of self-preservation, or the principle of avoiding suffering. Salecl (2000: 108) says: 'If psychoanalysis teaches us anything, it is that human beings are not inclined to achieve happiness. On the contrary, they find special enjoyment in suffering [...] – as beings of language, they are essentially marked by a force of self-annihilation, i.e. the death drive.' The old, grumpy Fredericksen stubbornly staying in his old house, even taking to violence, in order to stay true to the love of his life, is a simple example of this; he does not act to preserve himself, but to preserve his desire, and may even take some enjoyment from his grumpiness.

By having a speaking voice, the dog in *Up* exceeds its doggish state, enters into the chain of signifiers and relates to the big Other. The response to the order 'Speak!' exceeds the logic of the conditioned reflex, as one word (or signifier) takes the other in an unpredictable chain of speech. When Dug mechanically responds to the orders 'Sit!' and 'Shake!' Russell and Fredericksen are satisfied and smiling. But when he responds to the order 'Speak!' by actually having a human voice, they are shocked, as we now enter a territory beyond pure mechanist logic, the territory of language.

But the speaking dog is not only a figure of human language interrupting into the mechanical, it is also a figure that points to a mechanical aspect of human language. The speaking dog points back to the scene in which Russell at first knocks on Mr Fredericksen's door, reading the lines from his 'Wilderness Explorer's Handbook': 'Good afternoon. My name is Russell. And I am a Wilderness Explorer in Tribe 54, Sweat Lodge 12. Are you in need of any assistance today, sir?' Here Russell's speech seems completely as exterior and mechanical as if it had been put into him by an electronic necklace, clearly showing that also in the human being language can be some kind of record playing, some kind of prefabricated lines that the subject steps into and performs.

The cone of shame

In *Up*, the dog's voice is his master's voice. Visually there is an allusion to the image from the famous HMV trademark image, a painting of a dog listening to his master's voice emanating from the gramophone trumpet. The model for the painting was actually listening to his dead master's voice, the recorded voice of the painter's late brother, to whom the dog originally belonged. In *Up* there is no gramophone trumpet, but there is an object of a similar shape: 'the cone of shame'. This is a flea collar into which the dogs put a fellow dog when it has transgressed the rules of the community (at first Dug has to wear the cone of shame, at the end Alpha). Confirming Lacan's idea that language has its origin in objects taken out

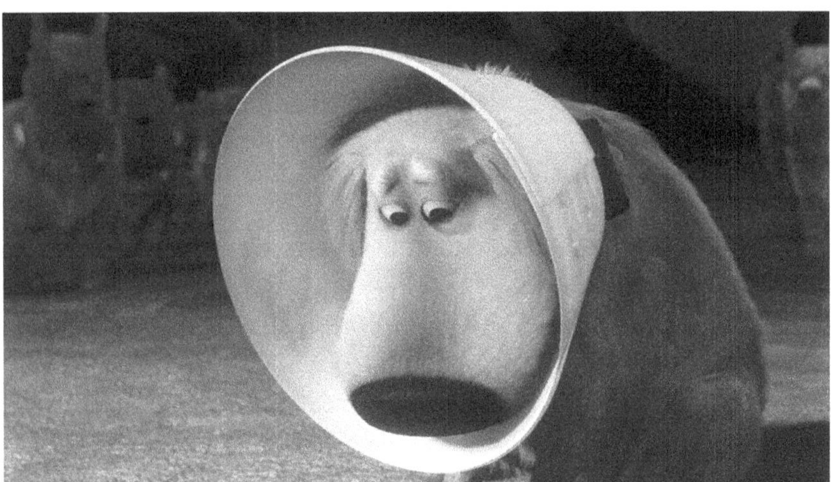

Figure 15 The cone of shame. From *Up* (Pete Docter, 2009) © Walt Disney Pictures/ Pixar Animation Studios.

of use ('vases made to remain empty, shields too heavy to be carried, sheaves that will dry out, lances that are thrust into the ground' (Lacan 2006: 225)), the cone has lost its use function and become a signifier, the signifier of shame.

Compared with the gramophone trumpet in the image of 'His Master's Voice', the cone in *Up* is inverted. In HMV it is opening towards the dog, putting him in the position of the receiver. In *Up* it is opening outwards from the dog, putting him (if the analogy to the trumpet is retained) in the position of the emitter. The echo of the HMV image in *Up* makes us see something like a double exposure, pointing to the voice as something induced into the subject as well as emitted from it. In the HMV image the master's voice is talking from without the dog, in *Up* it is talking from within. Or rather, in *Up* we are kind of confused about the place from which the dogs' voices are speaking: they seem at once to be put into the dogs from without, and to be inner voices extracted or amplified.

The trumpet of his master's voice converted into the cone of shame might also tell us something about the connection between master and shame. Shame is constitutive of the subject as being the object of the big Other. This is a point from Jean-Paul Sartre (the chapter on 'The Look' in *Being and Nothingness*). Having a human consciousness means feeling watched by the big Other means feeling shame. Shame is about being an object for the Other's gaze, as we know it already from Genesis – as soon as Adam and Eve have eaten the forbidden apple, they feel watched and cover their naked bodies. God as an *acousmêtre* calls out for Adam: 'Where are you?' Adam answers by talking about the fear provoked by his feeling naked, which we might understand as shame. As Žižek points out, the human subject is a being able to feel shame even when all alone. When, for instance, I stumble and fall while all alone in my apartment, I would still say 'oops'. To whom? To the big Other! (Žižek 2006: 25).

The electronic necklaces in *Up* actually at once function as voice and as instruments of supervision. Through the necklaces the dogs have their voices from their master at the same time as he is able to monitor them. The fact that the image of 'His Master's Voice' is implicitly present in the image of the cone of shame, points to this connection between big Other (here as *acousmêtre*) and shame.

Dogs and love

But what does Dug actually say? Who or what is talking through his electronic collar? What kind of speech animates him? There is something compulsive about

Dug's speech, as if he is subjected to a compulsion to speak out his mind, to say out loud what would normally just be a silent interior monologue, or even something beneath the level of consciousness: 'I can smell you', 'My master is good and smart', 'I have just met you and I love you', 'I will bring home the bird and you will like me', 'I love you now like I love my master', 'I like you temporarily' (!), 'I do not like the cone of shame', 'I was hiding under your porch because I love you.' Dug's statements are generally directed to his (replaceable) master, declaring his love and asking for love and recognition. In one sense it seems like a translation of doggish talk into human language, or rather what humans imagine a dog would say if it had language. It partly resembles the language of Lacan's dog Justine who speaks due to some inner pressure. But contrary to Lacan's dog, Dug actually seems capable of transference (he replaces one master by another), and his demand for love and recognition also seems (as it may even do in a real dog) very human.

The translation of doggish statements into verbal, human language will always make them exceed their doggishness; the very fact that the signifier is at play puts the dog into a dynamics of circulation, deference and address, that in itself exceeds the doggish logic of fulfilling needs rather than satisfying desire.

The domesticated dog's need for a master (for someone to feed and shelter it) is something else other than the human subject's being in dialogue with a master (the Other) whose desire he tries to decipher. To Lacan, desire actually arises out of the discrepancy between the subject's (satiable) 'appetite' for food (or other objects of need) and her (insatiable) demand for love. The infant cries for love and food, and when it has been fed it still cries – for love: 'This is why desire is neither the appetite for satisfaction nor the demand for love, but the difference that results from the subtraction of the first from the second, the very phenomenon of their splitting (*Spaltung*)' (Lacan 2006: 580).

This splitting does not exist within the dog, which loves (and feels loved by) the one who feeds him. As Salecl puts it: 'In Pavlov's experiment the dog does not become troubled with the desire of the experimenter. Dogs do not question the desire of the Other. And this is what distinguishes them from human beings. However, this lack of any question about the desire of the Other is also what makes dogs more lovable than humans' (Salecl 2000: 113). After this statement, Salecl asks: 'Why are we so much in love with our pets?' But it seems to me that she has already given the answer: because they are more loveable, due to their lack of big Other. As she herself later puts it: 'The dog became man's best friend because man cannot be man's best friend' (2000: 113).

The love for the pet is important to the plot in *Up*, as it is Russell's (typical childish) desire for a pet that attaches the bird and later Dug to him and Fredericksen. The bird's maternal and Dug's unconditional attachment, both in some way automatic, may represent that kind of flawless love that human beings let their pets represent.

In his short story 'Herr und Hund' ('Bashan and I'), Thomas Mann gives an unforgettable portrait of his dog Bauschan. The whole story revolves around the dog's need and love for a master, and Mann's reluctance to take on this role. The story is nearly able to convince even a Lacanian reader like myself that dogs are very human, not least when Mann tells how his dog was once himself the shameful object of love – he gives a wonderful description of the dog's complete unease when a sheep falls in love with it and will not give up on following it. The dog even seems exactly to doubt about the Other, about Mann's ability to be his master. This does not make of Mann the dog's big Other, though. Rather the opposite: Mann puts the dog in the place of the big Other. It is Mann who feels doubted by the dog. As an instance of the big Other, the dog poses to Mann the question about his identity and desire. Just like it is Pavlov's desire that makes his dog drool, it could be said to be Mann's desire that makes his dog doubt him.

But why is it, from a Lacanian point of view, so important to maintain the divide between human and animal? Actually, the important thing to maintain is that it makes a difference to be a *parlêtre*, a being of language, inhabited by and inhabiting in the chains of signifiers. The importance is not exactly where the divide is between *parlêtres* and other kinds of living creatures; if somebody proves that dogs actually have a signifying system similar to human verbal language (that is, based on the principles of arbitrariness and difference) and thus should be included in the 'parlêtres', it does not relieve the importance of defining what it means to be a creature of language and desire as different from not being one. It is not really important whether the limit is represented by the dog or, say, the cockroach.

The weird and disturbing image of the talking dog is at odds with the make-believe fairy-tale aesthetics represented by the multicoloured dimension of the film: the balloons, Kevin's feathers, the embroidered badges on Russell's belt. The multicoloured dimension seems to transform the lack and the Thing at the core of human existence into fullness and happiness. Mortality can be escaped by the means of multicoloured balloons, the skeleton (as which the bird is first presented) is covered by multicoloured feathers, and the monstrous, motherly

Thing turns out to be a multicoloured, caring bird mother. If Russell's belt of multicoloured badges is marked by a lack, the aim of the plot is not to make him accept this lack, but to fill it out by another multicoloured badge, even if, it must be said, the 'Ellie badge' that finally fills the lack, is odd and aesthetically less perfect than the others.

The force of *Up* is the bizarre and interesting image of the dog animated by a voice which is at once its master's and its own, like Žižek depicting the human voice as an alien inhabiting the body, and even more: defining humanity as this very being inhabited by an alien.

Epilogue: Animation and Capitalism

In the 1940s Sergei Eisenstein found in Disney a relief, a Utopian freedom from the society of mechanization and standardization as which he regarded America. In the 'plasmaticness' of the Disney figures, in their aptness for metamorphosis he sees an emancipatory potential, as when when Mickey Mouse sings, and his body and limbs stretch and grow to follow the tune. Or when in *Merbabies* (1938) the submarine creatures transform into earthly circus animals: the striped fish into a tiger, the octopuses into elephants. To Eisenstein, these metamorphoses represent an 'escape from yourself, from the once and for all fixed norms of form and behavior' (Eisenstein 2011: 12). In the animated ducks and mice he sees not only the humanization of animals, but also what he, seemingly anticipating Gilles Deleuze, calls the 'becoming-animal' of the human being and sees as a liberation from mechanical into sensory life (51).

Eisenstein stresses the temporariness of the freedom to be found in Disney, it is only for a moment: 'A short, fictitious, comic liberation from the clock work of American life' (2011: 17). Still, he does not see it as escapism, as opium for the people. Disney's cartoons are not 'golden lie dreams', but 'stains of sun', flickering, warming, ungraspable (10–11). They realize the want to be 'something else, something impossible' (13), whereas one might guess that what Eisenstein calls 'golden lie dreams' would be fictions that pretend that you can find freedom within the existing system, and not by breaking out from it.

To Eisenstein, Disney is 'a wonderful lullaby, for the suffering and the miserable, the humiliated and deprived', that is for the people living in capitalist America, where human life has become 'more merciless than in the stone age, more damned than in prehistoric times, and more enslaved than in the era of slavery' (2011: 39).

Contrary to Adorno, who scorned the cult of Mickey Mouse, Eisenstein, more in the manner of Walter Benjamin, sees a potentially liberating promise of happiness in Disney's art. When the American proletariat has won, he writes, 'they will raise no monument for Disney, neither in their hearts, nor in their streets and squares', but they will be thankful to the man who gave them 'breathing spaces' while they fought to survive in the merciless 'social paradise' of democratic America (2011: 10).

To Eisenstein, animation of the animal is also an animalization of the human being, pointing to a human existence freed of fixation and slavery. But what if the animated figure is a thing (a toy, a robot, a car) – do we then not risk a reification of the human being? Do we not enter into the dialectics of 'personification of things and reification of persons' that Marx critically pointed out in his *Capital* (Marx 1990: 209)? Animation and reification also go together in Eisenstein's example from *Alice in Wonderland*: right after Alice has obeyed the prosopopeia giving voice to a small thereby animated bottle, 'Drink me!', she feels herself to be 'shutting up like a telescope'. Alan Ackerman writing on *Toy Story* and Barbara Johnson writing on the trope of animation lean on Marx's view of the commodity as an animated thing.

The animate commodity

Alan Ackerman, in his analysis of *Toy Story*, relates animation to the commodity, reminding us of Walter Benjamin's definition of 'aura' as the ability of the inanimate object to return the human gaze, in other words some kind of animation of the inanimate (Ackerman 2011: 101, Benjamin 1968: 220–2). Ackerman's point is that the toys of *Toy Story*, by being animated, gain the 'aura' that makes of the commodity a fetish, following Marx's definition of the commodity: 'a very strange thing, abounding in metaphysical subtleties and theological niceties' (Marx 1990: 163). The toys become such 'strange things', perfect commodities to be sold as Pixar merchandise.

In that context it is interesting that one of the first Pixar shorts, *Red's Dream* (John Lasseter, 1987), presents its protagonist as a commodity on sale: the unicycle Red is standing in the corner of the bike shop, marked with a '50% off' tag. The devaluation of the commodity is compensated for by its animation, thus seeming to confirm Ackerman's idea that animation and valuation of the commodity go together. The unicycle is provided with a mind as the camera dives into its saddle and shows us the dream going on there.

In capitalist society the animation of things also has something to do with the fetishizing the commodity. As Barbara Johnson shows, there is in Marx a correlation between the animation of the commodity and the reification of the person. Johnson sums it up like this: '[O]ne transfers the social character of labor into a sociability among objects, sucking the humanness out of the makers and injecting it into the products' (Johnson 2008: 21). In the history of animation film this corresponds to the machine-like work of monotonous drawing that it has taken to animate the things and animals of cartoons. Johnson sees the advent of computer animation as the complete dismissal of the human hand, the animating work being done by a machine. She regards *Toy Story* as 'the perfect combination of the fantasy of childhood animism with the animation done by machines [. . .] [S]omething comes to life on one side, and becomes inanimate on the other' (2008: 170).

Pixar, though, belongs to a third-phase capitalism, in which the qualities wanted from the workers are creativity and team building rather than mechanical labour. The creative team of odd creatures is a recurring Pixar theme (the bunch of toys in *Toy Story*, the troupe of bugs in *A Bug's Life*, the team of monsters in *Monsters University*), and rather than sucking the human qualities out of the Pixar workers and injecting it into their characters, it seems to me to mirror the kind of work that went into the making of the films. The founders of Pixar, Ed Catmull and John Lasseter, stress the 'unique energy' of the group, the 'sense of community' and 'collective problem-solving' as major values of their staff (Paik 2007: 22, 14, 46).

Barbara Johnson points to the fact that a very common device to animate the commodity, with a very clear commercial aim, is what you in stylistics call 'prosopopeia', the figure of putting a voice into the thing, making it speak: 'A speaking thing can sell itself; if the purchaser responds to the speech of the object, he or she feels uninfluenced by human manipulation and therefore somehow not duped. We are supposed not to notice how absurd it is to be addressed by the Maalox Max bottle, or Mr. Clean, or Mrs. Butterworth, or the Quaker Oats man, or Aunt Jemina, or the Elidel man, or the Aflac duck' (Johnson 2008: 19).

This may support Ackerman's point that the animation – including the voicing – of the figures in *Toy Story* make them perfect commodities. In the *Toy Story* films the commodification of the figures is actually an important theme and plot device, like Buzz Lightyear's break down in *Toy Story* when watching a TV commercial and realizing that he is a mass-produced toy. His reaction is very touching and human, a deep existential crisis. But following Johnson one might argue that it is exactly the very humanity of Buzz, as distinct from the thingness of the shelved Buzz Lightyears in the commercial, that ensures his aura as a commodity. At the same time as Buzz's 'thingness' seems to say something about the human condition (in some aspects we are all mass-produced toys, clinging to the illusion of a unique personality), his humanity seems to say something about the aura of the commodity.

Johnson's illustration of prosopopeia is a talking Barbie. To make Barbie talk you have to push a pink button in the middle of her back. Johnson argues that this button replaces (and thus is associated with) the nipples and sexual organs that Barbie does not have, thus associating vocal with sexual organ. (Something similar happens in *Toy Story 3*, when the villains' violent introduction of a screw driver into Buzz Lightyear's back in order to change his voice has the air of sexual violation.) Barbie's sentences are 'about partying after the game on the weekend or some other fixture of high school life in the United States' (Johnson 2008: 18–19). Mattel (Barbie's production firm) had to draw back one sentence, though: 'Math is hard' (!). Perhaps it is partly in response to this that Pixar in *Toy Story 3* lets Barbie speak out a quite complicated political sentence when animating her crowd of toys to rebellion: 'Authority should derive from the consent of the governed, not from the threat of force.' Perhaps Mattel should adapt this idea; a clever, political talking Barbie might be the future way to assure her success as a commodity.

Other worlds?

Eisenstein connects Disney's transformative power to the line drawing – the line stretching and developing, outgrowing any fixed form. Computer animation is not based on the line, but on geometrical forms, combinable and multipliable. They do not work with the line, but rather with the texture. The aesthetic appeal of computer-animated images resides in a plasticity of surface rather than in the plasticity of the line. We do not find transformation as a recurring theme in Pixar's movies (although Elastigirl and Jack-Jack the fire baby may be late heirs to Disney's plasmaticness the Eisenstein way), but we do find other possible worlds, which is what computer animation creates. And we do find these impossible perspectives that only a camera freed from a human body can give us, like the shot from within Woody's sleeve (*Toy Story 2*), or the close up of Buzz Lightyear's face mirrored in the toddler's tongue (*Toy Story 3*).

One might ask whether Pixar sufficiently profits from the new medium's independence from the existing world, the fact that computer animation creates its own universe from nothing. Could not Pixar's worlds be more alternative to ours? Could not they, to a higher degree, create other possible worlds instead of taking such efforts in reproducing the one that we know? Is it not a bit like the situation at the end of the nineteenth century, lamented by Walter Benjamin: new techniques made it possible to build in a new material, iron, but what was built? Train stations resembling gothic cathedrals; there was a lack of imagination to let the new medium produce new figures and forms.

Paradoxically, computer animation seems to be more interested in rendering reality than in unfolding the virtual. Friedrich Kittler noticed as a commentary to the skin of the dinosaurs in *Jurassic Park* (Steven Spielberg, 1993) that 'computer generated films [. . .] do not try to compete with the fur coats in Hans Holbein's *The Ambassadors*' (Kittler 2002: 184). This was true for the first Pixar films, choosing for protagonists creatures with no fur nor hair: toys made of plastic, or bugs. But as Jens Schröter has noticed, rendering fur was the technical focus of the third Pixar film, *Monsters, Inc.* The gang of computer guys have made it into a sport to render those aspects of reality that are hardest to imitate in computer graphics, to the degree that makes it part of the film critic's pleasure to 'figure out what technical challenge the filmmakers have set themselves this time' (Thompson and Bordwell 2006, Schröter 2014: 38).

In a dialectical way computer animation may sometimes seem to bring us closer to the real by way of its virtuality. The computer animators have to study in detail the structure and functioning of the materials they imitate, be it skin, fur, hair, water, textile, drool. Thus hyper-reality becomes 'hyper' more in the sense of 'maximal' than 'beyond'. In Lacanian terms one might wager the thesis that virtual reality has the possibility to bring us closer to the real (as distinct from 'reality' meaning the symbolic order).

So, perhaps the special quality of computer animation is not to break with reality or media or genres as we know them, but to reflect upon them, and on its own construction of them. The Pixar films reproduce not only reality, but also the media and genres to which they are heirs. As Jens Schröter points out, the imagery of Pixar both refers to the tradition of photography and live action film, and to the tradition of drawing and painting, its imagery is 'hybrid' (Schröter 2014: 37).

Constructing forms and images out of nothing is different from reproducing them, it involves a special reflection on these forms and images. Thus Pixar's films are characterized by a high degree of self-reflection, making simulators, screens, projections, drawings, recurring themes. Constructing reality implies reflection on the process of construction itself, and the difficulty of setting a clear limit between construction and reality. As Malte Hagener puts it: 'Is a cowboy doll animated by a boy on the background of a sky painted on tapestry more or less constructed than Spencer Tracy on the background of a Bluescreen?' (Hagener 2014: 50).

Altogether the medium of computer animation is characterized by hyper-reality, reflexivity and hybridity. Especially, the self-reflexive quality has been of interest to this study, animation reflecting upon animation, but also the hyper-real quality has been an issue in the close reading of the repair scene from *Toy Story 2* and the drool scene from *Toy Story 3*.

Disney-fire, Pixar-volt

Eisenstein compares Disney to fire, the plasmatic element of transformation. Eisenstein's Disney-fire has an echo in Halberstam's 'Pixar-volt', the subversive energy that she finds in the alternative space and temporality of computer-animated films as well as in their cast of odd and oppositional communities.

Have I found Pixarvolt in Pixar's films?

I do agree with Halberstam that Pixar films sometimes contain Pixarvolt, and sometimes do not. I do not, though, make romance and family the dividing line between volt on/volt off. I find 'volt' in the exploration of creative sadism (*Toy Story 3*), the split between the eye and the gaze (*Toy Story 2*), the opting for the hysterization of education (*Monsters, Inc.*), the going with the death drive (*Finding Nemo*), the pun (*A Bug's Life*), the dystopia of totalitarian capitalism and enjoyment (*Wall-E*), the voice as an alien (*Up*), the mocking of Pavlovian behaviourism (*Up*) and the image of the soul as a rat (*Ratatouille*). I find non-volt in family ideology and vigilantism (*The Incredibles*), conforming to the Other (*Finding Nemo*), sustaining paternal desire (*Cars*), the cult of emotion (*Toy Story 3*, *Finding Nemo*) and multicoloured make-believe (*Up*).

First and last I find philosophical 'volt' in the self-reflectivity of the Pixar films that makes of animation not only a technical, but also an existential issue. As different answers to the question; What animates the human being? the films give us interesting suggestions. I hope that Lacan has helped highlight these suggestions, and that the Pixar films have helped highlight Lacan's concepts and notations.

References

Ackerman, A. (2011), *Seeing Things: From Shakespeare to Pixar*, Toronto, Buffalo, London: University of Toronto Press.

Andersen, H. C. (2004 [1837]), 'The Little Mermaid', in *Fairy Tales*, trans. Tiina Nunnally, London: Penguin Books.

Badiou, A. (2000), 'What is Love?', in R. Salecl (ed.), *Sexuation*, Durham, NC: Duke University Press.

Badiou, A. (2013), *Logics of Worlds*, trans. by Alberto Toscano, London: Bloomsbury.

Baudelaire, C. (1853), 'Morale du joujou', in *Le Monde littéraire*, 17 April.

Beckman, K. (2010), *Crash: Cinema and the Politics of Speed and Stasis*, Durham, NC: Duke University Press.

Benjamin, W. (1968 [1936]), 'The Work of Art in the Age of Mechanical Reproduction', in *Illuminations*, trans. Harry Zohn, New York: Schocken Books.

Benjamin, W. (1977 [1925]), *The Origin of German Tragic Drama*, trans. John Osborne, London: NLB.

Bergson, H. (1999 [1900]), *Laughter: An Essay on the Meaning of the Comic*, Copenhagen and Los Angeles: Green Integer Books.

Bion, W. R. (1962), *Learning From Experience*, London: William Heinemann.

Butler, R. (2007), 'Allegories of Animation: *Schindler's List*, *E.T.* and *The Lion King*', in Cholodenko, A. (ed.), *The Illusion of Life II: More Essays on Animation*, Sydney: Power Publications.

Cavarero, A. (2000), *Relating Narratives. Storytelling and Selfhood*, London and New York: Routledge.

Chion, M. (1992), 'The Impossible Embodiment', in Žižek, S. (ed.), *Everything You Always Wanted to Know about Lacan, but Were Afraid to Ask Hitchcock*, London/New York: Verso.

Chion, M. (1999), *The Voice in Cinema*, trans. Claudia Gorbman, New York: Columbia University Press.

Cholodenko, A. (ed.) (1991), *The Illusion of Life: Essays on Animation*, Sydney: Power Publications.

Cholodenko, A. (ed.) (2007), *The Illusion of Life II: More Essays on Animation*, Sydney: Power Publications.

Cholodenko, A. (2008), 'The Spectre in the Screen', in *Animation Studies Online Journal* vol. 3, http://journal.animationstudies.org/category/volume-3/spectre-in-the-screen/ (accessed 30 April 2015).

Chow, R. (1993), 'Postmodern Automatons', in R. Chow, *Writing Diaspora: Tactics of Intervention in Contemporary Cultural Studies*, Bloomington: Indiana University Press.

Crafton, D. (1982), *Before Mickey: The Animated Film, 1898–1928*, Cambridge, MA: MIT Press.

Eisenstein, S. (2011), *Disney*, trans. and ed. O. Bulgakowa and D. Hochmut, Berlin: Potemkin Press.

Freeman, E. (2005), '*Monsters, Inc.*: Notes on the Neoliberal Arts Education', in *New Literary History*, vol. 36, no. 1.

Freud, S. (1953 [1900]), 'The Interpretation of Dreams', in *Standard Edition of the Complete Psychological Works of Sigmund Freud*, vols IV–V, trans. and ed. J. Strachey, London: The Hogarth Press.

Freud, S. (1955a [1913]), 'Totem and Taboo', in *Standard Edition of the Complete Psychological Works of Sigmund Freud*, vol. XIII, trans. and ed. J. Strachey, London: The Hogarth Press.

Freud, S. (1955b [1918]), 'From the History of an Infantile Neurosis [The Wolfman]', in *Standard Edition of the Complete Psychological Works of Sigmund Freud*, vol. XVII, trans. and ed. J. Strachey, London: The Hogarth Press.

Freud, S. (1955c [1919]), 'The Uncanny', in *Standard Edition of the Complete Psychological Works of Sigmund Freud*, vol. XVII, trans. and ed. J. Strachey, London: The Hogarth Press.

Freud, S. (1955d [1919]), 'Beyond the Pleasure Principle', in *Standard Edition of the Complete Psychological Works of Sigmund Freud*, vol. XVIII, trans. and ed. J. Strachey, London: The Hogarth Press.

Freud, S. (1966 [1895]), 'Project of a Scientific Psychology', in *Standard Edition of the Complete Psychological Works of Sigmund Freud*, vol. I, trans. and ed. J. Strachey, London: The Hogarth Press.

Hagener, M. (2014), 'Das Leben der Dinge: Pixar und die digitalen Transformationen des Films', in J. Wende (ed.), *FILM-KONZEPTE 33: John Lasseter*, Munich: Edition Text + Kritik.

Halberstam, J. (2007a), 'Forgetting Family: Queer Alternatives to Oedipal Relations', in G. E. Haggerty and M. McGarry (eds), *A Companion to Lesbian, Gay, Bisexual, and Queer Studies*, Oxford: Blackwell Publishing.

Halberstam, J. (2007b), 'Pixarvolt – Animation and Revolt', online in FlowTV 606, vol. 6, http://flowtv.org/?p=739 (accessed 29 September 2014).

Hegel, G. W. F. (1997 [1807]), *Phenomenology of Spirit*, trans. A. V. Miller, Oxford: Clarendon Press.

Hoffmann, E. T. A. (1992), 'The Sandman', in R. Robertson (trans. and ed.), *The Golden Pot and Other Tales*, 85–118, Oxford: Oxford University Press.

Johnson, B. (2008), *Persons and Things*, Cambridge, MA and London: Harvard University Press.

Kittler, F. (2002), 'Computergrafik: Eine halbtechnische Einführung', in *Paradigma Fotografie*, (ed.) H. Wolf, Frankfurt/M: Suhrkamp Verlag.

Klein, M. (1998a [1933]), 'The Early Development of Conscience in the Child', in M. Klein, *Love, Guilt, and Reparation and Other Works 1921–1945*, London: Vintage.

Klein, M. (1998b [1925]), 'A Contribution to the Psychogenesis of Manic-Depressive States', in M. Klein, *Love, Guilt, and Reparation and Other Works 1921–1945*, London: Vintage.

Klein, M. (1998c [1940]), 'Mourning and its Relation to Manic-Depressive States', in M. Klein, *Love, Guilt, and Reparation and Other Works 1921–1945*, London: Vintage.

Kleist, H. von (1986 [1810]), 'Über das Marionettentheater', in *Sämtliche Erzählungen und andere Prosa*, Stuttgart: Reclam.

Kohut, H. (1971), *The Analysis of the Self*, Chicago: University of Chicago Press.

Lacan, J. (1979), *The Four Fundamental Concepts of Psychoanalysis*, trans. Alan Sheridan, London: Penguin Books.

Lacan, J. (1988), *The Ego in Freud's Theory and in the Technique of Psychoanalysis*, The Seminar of Jacques Lacan, Book II, New York: Norton.

Lacan, J. (1992), *The Ethics of Psychoanalysis, 1959–1960*, The Seminar of Jacques Lacan, Book VII, trans. Dennis Porter, London: Tavistock/Routledge.

Lacan, J. (1998), *On Feminine Sexuality: The Limits of Love and Knowledge*, The Seminar of Jacques Lacan, Book XX, trans. Bruce Fink, New York and London: Norton.

Lacan, J. (2006), *Écrits: The First Complete Edition in English*, trans. Bruce Fink, New York: W. W. Norton & Company.

Lacan, J. (2007), *The Other Side of Psychoanalysis*, The Seminar of Jacques Lacan, Book XVII, trans. Russell Grigg, New York and London: Norton.

MacCannell, J. F. (2000), *The Hysteric's Guide to the Future Female Subject*, Minneapolis and London: University of Minnesota Press.

Mann, T. (2003 [1919]), *Bashan and I*, trans. Herman George Scheffauer, Philadelphia, PA: Pine Street Books.

Marx, K. (1990 [1867]), *Capital: A Critique of Political Economy*, vol. 1, trans. Ben Fowkes, New York: Penguin.

McGowan, T. (2007), *The Real Gaze: Film Theory after Lacan*, Albany, NY: State University of New York Press.

Merleau-Ponty, M. (1968 [1964]), *The Visible and the Invisible*, Evanstone, IL: Northwestern University.

Mulvey, L. (1975), 'Visual Pleasure and Narrative Cinema', in *Screen* 16 (3), 6–18, Oxford: Oxford University Press.

Ngai, S. (2005), *Ugly Feelings*, Cambridge, MA: Harvard University Press.

Paik, K. (2007), *To Infinity and Beyond! The Story of Pixar Animation Studio*, London: Virgin Books.

Proust, M. (1988 [1913]), 'Combray', *Du coté de chez Swann*, (ed.) Antoine Compagnon, Paris: Gallimard Folio Classique.
Salecl, R. (2000), *(Per)versions of Love and Hate*, London and New York: Verso.
Santner, E. (2006), *On Creaturely Life*, Chicago and London: University of Chicago Press.
Santner, E. (2011), *The Royal Remains: The People's Two Bodies and the Endgames of Sovereignty*, Chicago and London: University of Chicago Press.
Sartre, J-P. (2001 [1943]), *Being and Nothingness: a Phenomenological Essay on Ontology*, trans. H. E. Barnes, New York: Citadel Press.
Schiller, F. (2004 [1801]), *On the Aesthetic Education of Man*, trans. Reginald Snell, New York: Dover Publications.
Schröter, J. (2014), 'Narration und Bildlichkeit in MONSTERS, INC.', in J. Wende (ed.), *FILM-KONZEPTE 33: John Lasseter*, Munich: Edition Text + Kritik.
Shakespeare, William (2003 [1603]), *Hamlet*, (ed.) H. Jenkins, The Arden Shakespeare, London: Thomson.
Sophocles (2011 [442 BC]), *Sophocles' Antigone*, trans. and ed. Diane J. Rayor, New York: Cambridge University Press.
Telotte, J. P. (2010), *Animating Space: From Disney to Wall-E*, Lexington: University of Kentucky Press.
Thompson, K. and Bordwell, D. (2006), 'Reflections on CARS', *8 October*, http://www.davidbordwell.net/blog/2006/10/08/reflections-on-cars/ (accessed 29 September 2014).
Truffaut, F. (1986), *Hitchcock: A Definitive Study of Alfred Hitchcock*, revised edition, New York and London: Simon and Schuster.
Verhaeghe, P. (1999), *Does the Woman Exist? From Freud's Hysteric to Lacan's Feminine*, trans. Marc du Ry, New York: Other Press.
Verhaeghe, P. (2000): 'The Collapse of the Function of the Father and its Effects on Gender Roles', in R. Salecl, *Sexuation*, Durham, NC: Duke University Press.
Wende, J. (2014), 'Spielzeug und Vergänglichkeit – letzte Dinge in den Filmen der TOY-STORY-Reihe', in J. Wende (ed.), *FILM-KONZEPTE 33: John Lasseter*, Munich: Edition Text + Kritik.
Winnicott, D. W. (1971), *Playing and Reality*, London: Tavistock.
Žižek, S. (1989), *Sublime Object of Ideology*, London and New York: Verso.
Žižek, S. (1991), *Looking Awry: An Introduction to Jacques Lacan through Popular Culture*, Cambridge, MA: MIT Press.
Žižek, S. (1992), 'In his Bold Gaze my Ruin is Writ Large', in S. Žižek (ed.), *Everything You Always Wanted to Know about Lacan, but Were Afraid to Ask Hitchcock*, London and New York: Verso.
Žižek, S. (1994), *The Metastases of Enjoyment: On Women and Causality*, London and New York: Verso.
Žižek, S. (1997), *The Abyss of Freedom: Ages of the World*. Ann Arbor: University of Michigan Press.

Žižek, S. (2005), 'Neighbors and Other Monsters: A Plea for Ethical Violence', in S. Žižek, E. L. Santner and K. Reinhard (eds), *The Neighbor: Three Inquiries in Political Theology*, Chicago: University of Chicago Press.
Žižek, S. (2006), *How to Read Lacan*, London: Granta Books.
Žižek, S. (2009), *The Monstrosity of Christ*, Cambridge, MA: MIT Press.

Filmography

Pixar films

A Bug's Life (John Lasseter and Andrew Stanton, 1998)
Cars (John Lasseter and Joe Ranft, 2006)
Cars 2 (John Lasseter and Brad Lewis, 2011)
Finding Nemo (Andrew Stanton and Lee Unkrich, 2003)
Lifted (Gary Rydstrom, 2006)
Monsters, Inc. (Pete Docter, David Silverman and Lee Unkrich, 2001)
Monsters University (Dan Scanlon, 2013)
Ratatouille (Brad Bird and Jan Pinkava, 2007)
Red's Dream (John Lasseter, 1987)
The Incredibles (Brad Bird, 2004)
Toy Story (John Lasseter, 1995)
Toy Story 2 (John Lasseter, Ash Brannon and Lee Unkrich, 1999)
Toy Story 3 (Lee Unkrich, 2010)
Up (Pete Docter and Bob Peterson, 2009)
Wall-E (Andrew Stanton, 2008)

Other

Blue Velvet (David Lynch, 1986)
Brazil (Terry Gilliam, 1985)
Hello, Dolly (Gene Kelly, 1969)
Life of Brian (Terry Jones, 1979)
Modern Times (Charles Chaplin, 1936)
Psycho (Alfred Hitchcock, 1960)
Pulp Fiction (Quentin Tarantino, 1994)
The Birds (Alfred Hitchcock, 1963)
The Conversation (Francis Ford Coppola, 1974)
The Great Dictator (Charles Chaplin, 1940)
The Matrix (Andy and Lana Wachowski, 1999)
The Pervert's Guide to Cinema (Sophie Fiennes, 2006)
Vertigo (Alfred Hitchcock, 1958)
Wild at Heart (David Lynch, 1990)

Index

www.ingramcontent.com/pod-product-compliance
Ingram Content Group UK Ltd.
Pitfield, Milton Keynes, MK11 3LW, UK
UKHW020124290926
15471UKWH00003B/278

9 781501 320170